LSD

LSD

Still With Us After All These Years

Edited by

Leigh A. Henderson

William J. Glass

LEXINGTON BOOKS
An Imprint of Macmillan, Inc.
New York

Maxwell Macmillan Canada
Toronto

Maxwell Macmillan International
New York Oxford Singapore Sydney

Library of Congress Cataloging-in-Publication Data

LSD : still with us after all these years / edited by Leigh A. Henderson, William J. Glass.
   p.   cm.
  Includes bibliographical references and index.
  ISBN 0-02-914395-0
  1. LSD (Drug)—United States. I. Henderson, Leigh A. II. Glass, William J.
HV5822.L9L73   1994
362.29'4—dc20   94-20172
                                                          CIP

Lexington Books
An Imprint of Macmillan, Inc.
866 Third Avenue, New York, N. Y. 10022
Maxwell Macmillan Canada, Inc.
1200 Eglinton Avenue East
Suite 200
Don Mills, Ontario M3C 3N1

Macmillan, Inc. is part of the Maxwell Communication Group of Companies.

Printed in the United States of America

printing number

1 2 3 4 5 6 7 8 9 10

Contents

LSD

Introduction

Leigh A. Henderson

William J. Glass

Lysergic acid diethylamide (LSD)—a drug synonymous with hippies, Haight-Ashbury, and the 1960s counterculture—has resurfaced as a public concern. Media attention has recently focused on LSD-related episodes in schools, seizures of LSD, and arrests of LSD dealers. Some newspaper articles from the mid-Atlantic region typify the nature of LSD resurgence into the public consciousness.

> For the first time that Baltimore County school officials can remember, two middle-school students have been expelled for possession of LSD. (*Baltimore Evening Sun*, February 19, 1992)

> Authorities seized 2,601 doses of LSD in several raids on what is considered the area's largest LSD distribution ring in two decades, police said. (*Richmond Daily Press*, April 12, 1992)

> Since a 14-year-old girl took two doses of LSD in a West Springfield high school bathroom this month, "wigged out" and eventually ended up charged with drug possession along with nine of her schoolmates, the nagging questions from parents haven't stopped. (*Washington Post*, April 27, 1992)

> In February, a 13-year-old Midlothian Middle School pupil was taken to a local hospital after he was found to be high on "blotter acid." . . . Another pupil at the school was charged with selling him a dose of the drug for $3.

1

"The interesting thing about LSD that we see is that it sticks mainly with kids—the 15-to-22 bracket," Lt. Proffitt said. (*Richmond News Leader*, May 4, 1992)

Newsweek, the *New York Times*, and the *Washington Post* have featured the "rediscovery" of LSD under such titles as "The New Age of Aquarius,"[1] "Use of LSD, Drug of Allure and Risk, Is Said to Rise,"[2] and "LSD: A Potent Trip."[3] In addition, LSD has figured prominently in several television news magazine shows, promoted with lines such as "It's back, and it's more dangerous than ever!" Is LSD indeed making a comeback?

The National Institute on Drug Abuse (NIDA) and the Drug Enforcement Agency (DEA) have taken these reports seriously. The DEA sponsored a conference on contemporary LSD use in December 1991 (in San Francisco, appropriately). Their findings are best expressed in the title of a publication distributed at that meeting: "LSD: It Never Went Away."[4] Prompted by renewed interest by the biomedical research community in LSD and other hallucinogenic drugs, NIDA convened a technical review on the basic action and pharmacokinetics of hallucinogens in July 1992. At the same time, NIDA sponsored the interdisciplinary series of studies on LSD that are the foundation for this book.

LSD exerts a fascination like no other drug. Although experience with it goes back fifty years, it remains one of the most poorly understood illicit drugs. LSD temporarily alters an individual's normal modes of perception, producing a flood of sensations. Colors and sounds become more intense, and subjective time is slowed. Visual illusions are characteristic, and these imagined or perceived images and movement may seem real. The emotional response can be one of euphoria and contentment or, less often, confusion, fear, anxiety, and despair. Some users believe that they achieve profound new insights into themselves, or even into the nature of God or the universe.

The appeal of drugs that tranquilize or sedate, such as narcotics and barbiturates, can be easily understood. We have all experienced times when we would like to close ourselves off, to make the world go away, or to relieve pain. Similarly, the appeal of drugs that keep us awake, dull our appetites, and seem to let us do more than we thought possible—drugs like cocaine, amphetamines, and even caffeine—is also comprehensible.

The appeal of LSD, however, remains elusive. Our five senses are the tools we use to interpret the world. LSD alters the way these senses, particularly sight and hearing, function. Thus, like the sensation of an earthquake, LSD undermines the stability of the world as we know it. In the most literal sense, if you cannot believe your eyes, what can you believe? A receptive user may welcome these novel perceptions and become more aware of how the senses function and their interrelationships. To others who try LSD, however, these alterations of the senses can be profoundly disturbing. And to a large public, reasons for desiring such sensations are simply incomprehensible.

It is difficult to fathom the LSD mystique without an understanding of the drug's past. LSD was introduced into the United States in 1948 as a psychiatric wonder drug. Dramatic claims were made for its supposed cathartic potential; proponents cited its ability to cause rapid personality and behavioral changes, thus saving countless hours of psychiatric therapy. The drug was hailed as a cure for everything from schizophrenia to criminal behavior, sexual "perversions," and alcoholism. By 1965 some 40,000 patients had received LSD as part of psychiatric therapy.

From this atmosphere of enthusiasm, LSD quickly escaped the confines of psychiatry. By 1962, pirated capsules were available in the street drug market, and illicit use exploded when legitimate manufacture was outlawed in 1965. LSD attained almost mythical stature in the late 1960s and early 1970s, aided by its association with such celebrity figures as Timothy Leary and Ken Kesey. Unlike other drugs of the time, it was initially used by highly educated, articulate individuals based on college campuses. They were able, in lectures and writings, to communicate effectively to others the LSD experience. Some observers found promises of visions of heaven in these accounts. To others, the same accounts more nearly resembled descent into hell. LSD rapidly captured the nation's imagination, attracting some and terrifying others.

The phenomenal interest in LSD reflected a confluence of social factors.[5] These included a record number of youths pursuing higher education and a heightened societal interest in the workings of the mind. During these years, part of a generation of young people adopted LSD and psychedelic experience as vital components of a counterculture that urged them to "turn on, tune in, and drop out." The counterculture was colorful, and many of its spokespersons were articulate; it attracted immense media attention. The numerous social histories of this period that focused on the role of LSD will not be retold here. Awareness of LSD's social context, however, is critical to an understanding of contemporary LSD use. Many of the current beliefs about and attitudes toward LSD were shaped by the often sensational stories that appeared in this period.

In the 1980s, LSD vanished from the nation's front pages, replaced in succession by cocaine, heroin, and crack. It appears as if the nation can interest itself in (or perhaps tolerate hearing about) only one drug problem at a time. As the media spotlight moved on, the spread of information about LSD—whether factual or embellished—ceased.

LSD, however, did not vanish from the drug scene. In the 1990s about as many high school students report use of hallucinogens during the past year as report using cocaine (see Chapter 4). Although substantial progress has been made in reducing use of cocaine and other drugs among adolescents, hallucinogen use is not declining. A small but persistent proportion of secondary school students and young adults find LSD attractive, as evidenced by regional outbreaks, anecdotal reports, and national surveys of students. Over the period 1977–1992, some 7 to 10 percent of each high school senior class has tried LSD at least once.[6] (Reliable estimates of the number of "old hippies" that continued use into middle age or later are unavailable; however, LSD use by adults appears to be minimal.)

Concerns about LSD will continue, especially as local media focus attention on use in the schools or report successful drug enforcement operations against LSD distribution networks. Some inexperienced users may encounter problems, alarming their parents, schools, and communities. It is important that those who are interested or concerned have access to the broad body of knowledge about LSD. Therefore it seems appropriate at this time to summarize what has been learned about LSD in the past and to synthesize this with an understanding of LSD use and its consequences today.

What has occurred over the past generation that can explain the movement of LSD from the college-based counterculture of the 1960s to the middle and high schools of today's suburbs? How dangerous is LSD? Can it cause permanent harm? Where does it come from? How is it sold? How is it used? Is its use spreading? What can we do about it? What *should* we do about it?

In the quest to understand LSD and its consequences, the editors of this book have developed an approach incorporating multiple sources of data and different methods of data collection that we believe yields a more vivid, complete, and credible picture of the LSD phenomenon. Too often assumptions about drug use are based on a single source, or similar sources, of data. Drug use is a complex phenomenon, and it is important to understand not only who uses drugs but why and how they use them, as well as the consequences of drug use. By using a combination of methods, different perspectives become evident. While any single perspective is limited, several perspectives together extend and reinforce each other, so that the whole is greater than the sum of its parts.

To understand the place that LSD occupies in today's society, we as editors have assembled perspectives from users, sellers, a law enforcement officer, and health researchers. In Chapters 1 and 5, qualitative data provide an in-depth look at one community's experience with LSD. There, federal officials broke up a distribution network supplying LSD to high school students and young adults; the episode received considerable local publicity and sparked renewed national media attention to LSD. Evidence uncovered in this and other local investigations led to the arrest in May 1993 of the head of a major national LSD organization. A DEA official has been quoted as saying that this group dominated the nationwide LSD market in 1991 and 1992, selling an alleged two million doses a month over the two-year period.

For Chapter 1, ethnographic study methods were employed in interviewing adolescent LSD users and their parents. In their own words, the users recall their experiences (both good and bad) with the drug. We learn about why, how, where, and when LSD was experienced, its anticipated and actual effects, and the problems that were eventually encountered. The parents' attitudes and knowledge about drugs in general and LSD in particular are presented in striking contrast to those of the adolescents.

A historical perspective is presented in Chapter 2. A comprehensive review of the medical, drug abuse/addiction, and social science literature highlights both past and recent scientific knowledge. The drug has been used in the United States, first medically and then illegally, for more than forty years. It was the subject of intense scientific interest and research until about 1980, when financial support for research dried up. Its nonmedical use began in the early 1960s. Thus some thirty years of scientific research into LSD and another thirty years of observation of its nonmedical use are available. This chapter defines LSD's unique position in the panoply of abused drugs: its history, its physiologic and psychologic effects, its marketing and distribution, and its relationship to the law.

Chapter 3 addresses the primary concerns of parents, teachers, and at least some users. What are the adverse consequences of LSD use? What are its short-term effects? Its long-term effects? Its psychiatric consequences? Can it cause cancer or birth defects? What about the sensational media stories that are part of LSD mythology—people staring at the sun until they go blind or tear their eyes out? Are they true? Chapter 3 uses the medical and drug abuse/addiction literature to address LSD's potential for adverse consequences. The myths are explored, and their grounding in fact is assessed.

For Chapter 4, we analyzed a variety of quantitative data sources to determine the extent of LSD use, to identify the core group of LSD users, and to explore the patterns of use over time. The sources included the National Household Survey on Drug Abuse,[7] Monitoring the Future: A Continuing Study of the Lifestyles and Values of Youth,[6, 8] and the Drug Abuse Warning Network,[9, 10] all sponsored by the Substance Abuse and Mental Health Services Administration or the National Institute on Drug Abuse; and the Drug Use Forecasting Project[11] sponsored by the National Institute of Justice. Through these sources we were able to extract information about LSD use among (1) representative samples of American households, (2) representative samples of secondary school students and young adults, (3) individuals treated in hospital emergency rooms for drug-related problems, and (4) individuals arrested for drug-related and other crimes.

These sources reveal the numbers and types of people who use LSD, when they started, when they stopped, and the medical emergencies they experienced. In addition to exploring characteristics of LSD users, their patterns of use, and discontinuation of use over time, Chapter 4 describes LSD use within the context of other drug use.

Chapter 5 describes, in the words of an undercover federal agent, a distribution network supplying LSD to high school students and young adults. The agent and his colleagues interviewed numerous LSD sellers and users in the pursuit of their investigations. We learn how a local LSD distribution network is established and how relatively unsophisticated dealers market and sell the drug and produce profits. The characters and motivations of the young adults involved are explored as the investigator recounts his interviews with the arrestees. The chapter concludes with a description of the effects of the trial and sentencing on the community, including the devastating consequences to the young LSD sellers.

LSD has recently received national attention as part of the ongoing debate over mandatory sentencing for drug offenders. Chapter 6 briefly discusses some of the legal issues surrounding LSD detection, possession, and distribution. Chapter 7 summarizes the results of the studies discussed earlier in the book, and it attempts to respond to the key questions about LSD use in the 1990s. Is use increasing or otherwise changing? What should be the major areas of concern posed by LSD use? Chapter 7 also addresses the implications for prevention of the information that has been presented.

This book incorporates clinical, epidemiologic, and social science research, and it presents different but related snapshots of LSD and LSD users. It is only when all the snapshots are viewed together that LSD use and its relative position in the larger picture of drug use becomes clear. We believe that this "holographic" approach, combining a historical perspective with quantitative and qualitative data, provides unique insights into the phenomenon that is LSD.

1

What Is a Trip— and Why Take One?

James MacDonald

Michael Agar

The best part? You feel so elated at times. I would sit there with a smile on my face for hours, until my muscles were hurting and I couldn't smile anymore, but I couldn't get that damn grin off of my face. I'd be really happy and think of the stupidest shit and it would be the most amazing things you'd ever thought of, stuff like that. Every time it was a different experience. It was never the same, ever. That's what I enjoyed most.

You know you've got control over your whole life, you know. You just see everything that's going to happen. I remember one time I was walking back to the store with my best friend, we're walking down the road, we're tripping, nice, mellow, no one around, nothing, barely any cars on the road. Nothing was bothering us or anything, you know we just said we wished we felt like this for the rest of our lives, just two best friends just walking down the road.

These are the voices of two former LSD users talking about their trips. Theirs and the voices of other adolescent users and their parents will be heard throughout this chapter. We emphasize their voices because the question that guided this study was as follows: "Why, from their own perspective, do young people use LSD?" Epidemiologic studies can reveal some characteristics of those who use LSD, and sociologic and clinical research can indicate correlates of use. But the answer to the question "Why?" requires an inquiry into the motivations and perceptions of the users themselves.

When the goal of research is to learn another point of view, an ethnographic approach is the appropriate one. This study is based on ethnographic interviews, where control over the flow of talk passes from the researcher to the interviewee. The principal researchers themselves conduct the interviews, but the goal of analysis is to identify patterns rather than to measure and correlate variables. Because the patterns are in the material rather than imposed on it, the presentation is structured by what people actually said, not as a set of categories illustrated by their speech.

We interviewed six adolescents (four boys and two girls) and two parents, all from the same suburban community near a large mid-Atlantic metropolitan area.* All the adolescents were seventeen years old at the time of the interviews and were enrolled in a drug rehabilitation program. All were former LSD users who had begun using the drug around the age of twelve. None of them used only LSD; all had been involved with other legal and illegal drugs as well, a fact that may confound the findings in ways left unexplored. The two parents we spoke with had adolescent children who had used LSD often.

We began with open, unstructured questions that changed over time as we learned from the youths and their parents. The emphasis was on listening, not asking. All interviews were tape-recorded, with full assurance of confidentiality to each interviewee. By analyzing the interview transcripts, we identified patterns in which particular segments of the interviews cohere and connect. They represent examples of common underlying themes.

When we talked with the adolescents, they often spoke about LSD trips. They talked about good trips, bad trips, first trips, and last trips. They also talked about the good and bad aspects of LSD, why they used it, and why they had quit. They talked about how LSD changed their worlds. The key theme, as the youths told it, is that LSD transforms reality. This theme, often unrecognized by adults—even professional drug researchers—runs throughout their

---

*To honor assurances of confidentiality, the names of the community and the interviewees are not revealed.

stories. They described cognitive distortions and dramatic changes in perception, information processing, and memory as the most salient features of the LSD experience. In the words of one interviewee, "That's what makes tripping tripping."

Underlying the following presentation is a simple but profound fact. To understand the *why* of LSD use, to understand the difference between the users and the adults, one must listen as the youths tell of their LSD experiences.

What Makes a Trip a Trip

There were a few things on which the adolescents were unanimous. The first and most prominent was that tripping on LSD is fun. They loved doing it. Every user talked about this, and some talked about it repeatedly.

> It was always so much fun. I mean, the Pink Floyd light show came to town, and so we got our acid and bought those funky glasses that they sold there in the stands that twist the light into different colors and whatnot. We just had fun sitting there watching the light show—laser light show. I was on like five and one-half hits. I was just enjoying myself.

> When I was using, I never thought I was escaping in any way. I just did it because it was fun. The rest of my life sucked, but this was fun. This was something I found that was fun, and I liked it.

> You see, acid to me made me think of fun. It didn't make me think about crimes or anything, it just made me feel spaced out. Like laughing and thinking everything's a joke. But if I'm drinking or doing some coke or weed, then I feel like maybe doing some crimes.

> I loved it. Just for all these reasons, it was such a fun drug. It was a unique drug. There was nothing else like it.

Tripping on LSD alters both perceptions and thinking. It can change the mundane world into a startling and amusing show. Situations that might normally be predictable and boring become unpredictable, interesting, and entertaining. If the familiar stunted house plant on the kitchen table suddenly says "Hello" and asks you for some water, something extraordinary is happening.

I mean, sometimes you could just sit there in one place the whole time you trip and see so many things that wouldn't be funny when you are not tripping that are so funny then.

Oh yeah, it's fun to trip in the city, too. We just walk up to a wall and look up and walk away slowly, and it will look like you're flying. 'Cause it looks like the building is going up off the ground, and you just stick your hands up and move away slowly, and it looks like you are off the ground and flying. We were in the city one time and there was a big giant wall, and it was like an old wall—and, you know, if you are on acid and you see something weird, you like to just sit there, you know, and see what that does. See if it does anything for you, and so we were just sitting there and it turned into a giant sponge, 'cause there was water on the top of it coming down a little bit, and then there was water on the bottom of it. So it looked just like this huge sponge, and it started getting closer and the pores would open up like a sponge, and we were just sitting there for like hours. And then once we started coming down, "Oh, take another hit." We had to watch it forever.

My friend and I were sitting watching a jeep. I lived over near a park, and there was a little driveway that went down the park, and there was a little bump and the driveway went down, and this jeep decided to come and go "foomp" and jump off, and they would get probably about seven or eight feet down before they hit the ground. It was really amusing just to sit there and watch them, because they'd go jump, three or four minutes later they'd be back again jumping, and it was this little Suzuki Samurai. I had so much fun.

When a person is tripping on LSD, everything is touched with a patina of mystery and magic. You never know what will happen next. But as you are experiencing these distortions and illusions, there is always the knowledge that they are just that: illusions. The person on LSD never completely loses sight of the fact that the distortions are drug induced; the altered world never completely supplants the real world one remembers. In fact, one must believe that when the drug wears off, things will return to normal. If the youth loses sight of this fact for too long, a bad trip—even a profoundly bad trip—may result.

There'll be moments when you think, you know, that it won't stop. And you'll just stay like this, you know, and what would happen if I stay like this, you know? Like a freak, you know, just walking around and seeing like, I don't know, like chairs like walking around and plants talking and stuff, you know? And that's what you think about, you know—"I'm going to end up like retarded in a hospital," like shaking and shit. But, you know, it'll get thrown out, you'll just get distracted by something else.

Tripping on LSD transforms perceptions not only of external objects and situations, but of oneself. Every interviewee mentioned some personal attribute or skill that he or she thought was enhanced by tripping.

Oh yeah, definitely your mind is like totally altered. When you're on acid, it's—your imagination is a lot thicker, you think a lot more things that you normally wouldn't think of. You see things and they trigger—you see one hallucination, and it'll like trigger so many ideas off that one thing. It seems like it just gets you thinking like crazy, you know, you can elaborate on so many ideas, it's weird.

I mean, I just feel whatever I'm thinking about before, whether it's an everyday thing. I drop a hit of acid and something's been on my mind all day, I can actually think about that out to its fullest extent. It feels like it just pulls something and lifts it out of me. My thinking—it feels like my thinking is just three times as good as it is, and makes me imaginative and wonder and dream and daydream a lot more.

And like with LSD, it just seemed to me that I couldn't function without it, you know, I couldn't be as perky and aware and deep and artistic or creative without it. That's how I saw myself.

[My friend] would show me something [on the guitar], or he'd have his own song, and I'd just make up something that would go with it, that just sounds so good that it would just blow me away, you know. I could always do that when I was on LSD, always. I mean, when I first started playing guitar when I was tripping, I had a hard time doing it just, you know, because it was mind-boggling, it was just like reading when I was tripping. And then I just got the hang of it, I just—it just came out easy, you know. I felt so great.

I have a sketch pad that almost all of the drawings in it are while I'm on acid, and they're fine, like the technique was—they look fine. They don't look like . . . they're just like things I was thinking. When I was stumped in art [class] a lot, I'd think, "Well, I'll just take a hit of acid, and I'll think of some good stuff to draw." That was the case a couple of times.

All agreed that the experience of a trip is fun, a change in perceptions of the world and oneself that renders life more interesting, less boring. They also all agreed that tripping is a shared experience that can provide the basis for close personal bonds.

If you like trip with somebody, then you get a good relationship with them. Somehow you just feel like you know each other now. Like my best friend and me tripped once, and that is how we became best friends. We just decided after that that we were good friends.

The youths also all believed that tripping created a world from which adults were excluded because they didn't understand what the kids knew about the world created by LSD. Adults represented a set of rules centered on stability, order, and predictability that made no sense at all during a trip. The adult world represented the problem that a trip was designed to solve.

I couldn't stand authority figures when I was tripping. I got really scared. Whether that was a parent, a librarian, cop, didn't matter. I didn't like adults when I was tripping.

In their descriptions of what it feels like to trip, the adolescents were in total agreement. But when they talked about what they did on a trip and where they did it, the uniformity in the interviews disappeared. Favorite tripping activities ranged across a wide spectrum. Some simply sat quietly in one place and watched the spectacle provided by the transformation of the regular world. Some went hiking or camping, or just wandered through the city. Some always tripped with the same small group of close friends; some with a larger, more amorphous group; and some went to parties. They tripped at home, in parks, at movies, in cars, and at shopping centers.

Sometimes we just do it for fun, like, "Hey, you want to trip?" And go somewhere and just journey, get backpacks full of beer and just drop a hit and just walk and walk and walk.

I would just sit and watch, that's what I liked to do when I tripped. I didn't like to go out and be with a lot of people.

People won't be sitting around conversing rapidly when we go out tripping. I know a couple of people that just can't keep their mouth shut when they're tripping, and they'll just go on and on and on. But most of the other people just tend to keep to themselves.

Well, there's kinds that go to parties; there's kinds that do it just on the weekends and like drive around and stuff. There's the kind of people that like go sit like one place like all night, just drinking and tripping, while there's other people that'll just like, I don't know, like take it after school, driving around. Some people that like go camping and stuff, and they'll do it. I don't know, there's probably a lot more.

These diverse locations, social groups, and activities do have some things in common. The social settings are all informal, unstructured, and supportive. The physical settings all provide a degree of unpredictability within a dependably safe framework. These are locations where a person is unlikely to meet or be forced to respond to hostility or authority. There is little likelihood that a threatening situation will develop that would require quick thinking for self-preservation.

A good trip, then, is an enjoyable experience. The boring, predictable external world turns adventurous and exciting, and the perception of one's own creativity is enhanced. A good trip forges social bonds among participants. Trips belong to the youths and establish a world in which adults have no expertise, a world that in many ways turns adult priorities upside down. Although situations for good trips vary, they all protect the user against immediately threatening problems so that the trip can take its unpredictable course without any cause for worry.

Bad Trips

During the interviews, the adolescents spent a great deal of time talking about good trips, but they also talked about bad ones. Bad trips are an accepted part of taking LSD, and all of them expected to have one occasionally. As one interviewee said, "Basically the way I looked at it was, you're gonna have a few bad trips, but you're also going to have a shitload of good ones." When they did have bad trips, they often explained it with one of two causes: either an underlying bad mood, or "bad acid."

I think if you have a bad day, then you trip, you probably most likely will have a bad trip. But if you have a good day and you're all jolly and stuff, then you'll have a good trip.

Then I still couldn't sleep, I was just so tired. And you know, sometimes if there is so much strychnine in it, in the LSD, it's just like I felt sick to my stomach. I couldn't eat anything, not for a long time—I mean just for like a day or a few hours, then it would be gone.

But while everyone expects an occasional bad trip, sometimes users have bad trips that reach truly nightmarish proportions. Four adolescents we talked with had experienced profoundly bad trips. By looking closely at three stories of such trips, it is possible to reach some conclusions about their causes that go beyond the explanations usually given by the adolescent users.

The third friend of mine had only taken two hits, he was trying to calm my other friend down who had taken his clothes off, and I was just sitting in the middle of the field. Somebody saw him running around naked and called the cops, and the cops came, and I don't remember a whole lot. I remember sitting in the middle of the field. There was a cop walking out towards me; I was just sitting there. He had his gun drawn, and he was moving back and forth like this, so there was a whole row of him in three different colors. It was like green, brown, red—yellow, brown, and green, I think. There was just a whole row of them and they were all doing this, and I was just sitting there. It didn't occur to me when I saw the pretty blue and red lights that something was happening. I remember seeing them beat the shit out of my best friend. It scared me a lot. Then when we got arrested—I just, I didn't know what was happening to me at all. I didn't have a good trip from start to finish. Even before the police came, I wasn't having a good trip.

My worst trip? I was at my best friend K.'s house, and his brother-in-law was over there. . . . His brother-in-law and his wife just got in a fight, and my girlfriend and her friend was over at K.'s house. My girlfriend's friend had messed around with K.'s brother-in-law, so that's why K.'s brother-in-law and his wife got into a fight, so we all got messed up except K.'s brother-in-law. He doesn't have it all, anyway. I freaked out, put myself in a closet. I strictly lost it—I landed outside a couple of times, you know, ran in the woods, got lost in the woods. But it was just that guy right there is what messed everything up. He's been in jail for manslaughter charges, assault charges, he's real crazy. So it just—I thought he was going to freak out and end up killing me or something, so I just lost it and that's all I was thinking about the whole night.

My feeling was like, "This is never going to stop," you know. I had no sensation of, like, that this was slowing down at all. Once it started, it was like I was peaking forever. It started, you know, hanging upside down, I was just like all clenched up, all sweaty, my hat was completely wet, and I was just shaking and watching this girl like that was like turning into a cat and her tail was fanning her off, and there was like pyramids and stuff behind her, and it was just like I couldn't really feel my body and I just had no control. The feeling was just shaky and there was so much tension, it was just scary, it was like so emotional. There was just too much emotion involved, and it was a really scary experience. Someone was supposed to pick her up and her parents were out of town, and we were upstairs and we kept hearing footsteps downstairs, like in her basement—and, I don't know, I mean, it turned out that someone had broken into her house.

[*Interviewer*: So it was real?]

Yeah, so it was real, and that makes it even more scary because we were, I mean, we were upstairs and looking out the windows. We could see all these people coming out of the bushes, but I don't think anyone was ever there, and it was just like, it was really, every time we tried to help each other out, it would just like fall apart.

Although these three bad trips seem different, they all have a single element in common: they all involve loss of control. During a good trip, cognitive distortion transforms the world into a fascinating display; it changes the usual and boring into the unpredictable and interesting. But the knowledge that it is an illusion is maintained, and the situation itself is protected and benign. During a bad trip this sense of control is lost. The users themselves often spoke of good and bad trips in relation to losing control. One adolescent said this about his reaction to people who were having bad trips:

You know they'd try to cover it up, but they were real nervous about everything. You know, always moving here or there, tapping their feet constantly, just always doing something, just, I don't know. I don't want to come straight out and say, you know, that you shouldn't be doing it, you're freaking out, because I was doing it and I'd be a hypocrite. You know, I mean, I'd be like, "You all right? You under control?" or something like that. "You shouldn't be doing as much as you're doing."

A person can lose control during a trip in two ways. The first is to lose the knowledge that the distortions are not real. The trip changes from an alternative reality to the only reality; one starts to think it will never end. The second way to lose control, even if one maintains the knowledge that the distortions are not real, is to lose control of the actual situation. The situation makes demands that cannot be met; circumstances require a level of awareness and directed response that is made impossible by the LSD. One believes oneself to be in serious trouble, but cannot understand what is happening well enough to react appropriately.

The irony is that one objective of a trip is to lose control, but loss of control is the cause of a bad trip. This is the narrow line that divides good trips from bad ones. Good and bad trips are not discrete categories, but rather two ends of a continuum. Trips can lie anywhere along the continuum, or can change character as they develop. The trick is to maintain enough control—although enough is a relative thing, determined by both the personal and the situational factors.

The continuum between good and bad trips appears in the following stories about trips in school. Every youth told such stories. School trips are potentially bad because the setting is highly structured, with authority figures in control to whom you must respond, and the activities demand clear perception, reasoning, and recall. You are asked to perform tasks at which you are destined to fail and from which you cannot escape.

> I can't read when I'm tripping, I can't write when I'm tripping. I mean it was just—instead of seeing one word, like one word across the line, I see that word over and over and over. And I try to read that one word, and I just keep skipping that word going across the line. It's real hard.

> I was tripping in school and you can't work in school, 'cause you look at the letters and they fall off the pages. And you try to pick it back up, but it doesn't work.

I remember being in geometry class once, taking a test, and I couldn't remember any of it. And like the words and like the images on the paper were like scrambling and stuff and like, there was stuff coming out of the paper, like really like twinkles and stuff. I was just thinking that the teacher's looking at me and going, "Jesus, what's wrong with this kid?" and it was just crazy. My friend said I was like writing in the air and stuff, and it was just really crazy.

All the youths told us that LSD and school did not mix, that the trip disabled the control they needed to function in that situation. Most concluded that school is not the place to trip, that it is a cause of bad trips that can be avoided. But for at least one, the slide into a potentially bad trip in school was an attraction; for him, the added danger added to his enjoyment of the trip.

The settings people preferred for tripping—like parks, shopping malls, and their own homes—were selected to guard against losing situational control. They were generally benign, unstructured, without authority figures, and with friends. Safety was seldom threatened. If the youths lost the ability to monitor and respond to the environment effectively, it made no difference; everything could be expected to move along in a safe, predictable way without any need for attention.

In the three bad trips described earlier, the youths were put into threatening situations where they were forced to make accurate assessments of their surroundings and produce logical and directed responses. This was not possible because of the LSD. In these situations, the level of distortion produced by the LSD made effective responses aimed at self-preservation impossible. Being accosted by a gun-wielding policeman is a difficult situation, but when the LSD produces six policemen in rainbow colors, all hope of control has been lost. Being in a house with a potentially homicidal maniac, or one that is being burgled, is a threatening situation made terrifying and impossible to handle because one couldn't trust one's perceptions or reasoning. In more benign settings, these trips might have been good, but the appearance of actual danger turned them profoundly bad.

In addition to situational factors, personal factors determine what an acceptable level of distortion will be. Each individual has his or her own personal tolerance. This is illustrated by the stories of the one interviewee who never had a good trip; he took LSD only a few times.

> I thought my dad was dead. And that my own people were going to kill me. And that's the bad trip that I had. The worst trip—and with other drugs I never felt that way, that my friends were going to kill me and my dad was dead. And suddenly I get up and started screaming, "Get me outta here!" And they were going to kill me and all this, and then suddenly I just started, you know—when you get down, you start getting down slowly off of acid. And then say I was getting down and then I just fell asleep, and I woke up and I said, "I'm never doing this shit."

This youth had a different background from the other interviewees. He is a Hispanic who grew up in a rough neighborhood of San Francisco, where he was a member of a street gang for four years. His family had moved to a suburban community four years before the interview. He described himself as being "very tight" with his friends and said, "Yeah, you always gotta watch your back."

Although he had used many drugs, the Hispanic youth did not like LSD. His main complaint was that it created too many "illusions." For him, the cognitive distortions produced by LSD were unacceptable at any level. It made being with his friends impossible because it interfered with his ability to monitor his own behavior accurately and to gauge his friends' reactions. It made him feel defenseless in what he perceived as a hostile and dangerous world.

> Let me put it this way, man. When you're snorting the stuff [cocaine] and you're going out and fighting everybody, then you know, say, me, I knew what was going on. But say I'm here in the room and I'm not doing nothing and I'm on acid. And then suddenly you are watching something and then think it's coming after you. You're imagining. Cocaine, you do not imagine, you just cope, you know?

Situational and personal factors contribute to a youth's determining what is enough control. The amount of LSD one takes also plays a crucial role. As the dose increases, so does the level of distortion it produces; as the distortion increases, so does the chance of a bad trip. Even an individual who has a high personal tolerance for distortion in a generally benign situation can lose control if the dose is too high. A heavy user relates this story about such a situation:

I was driving in a car and I was hearing music, and the radio wasn't even on and I was hearing all kinds of weird things, and it was just like I had never been so surrounded by like the hallucinations. It was like everything was altered; everything was shaking, moving, breathing. The walls were like smothering me, they were real close around my face, when really there was a twenty-foot radius like all around me. It was like everything was up close in my face, and just one thing led to another. I'd get paranoid, I'd go outside, and like trees were falling down and moving. It was like absolute destruction. It wasn't like when I'd usually trip, like everything was so like harmonized. It was like everything was nice and even, but this one was like really sporadic. It was like I had no grip on it at all; everything was just out of my control. It was like the world was falling apart, just insane. And that's why I decided that I wasn't going to do it anymore, because I had done my share and that was it. I just didn't want to see that again.

Profoundly bad trips can cause a user to quit. The users' motivation for taking LSD is that they love the experience—but the fear of having another profoundly bad experience can overwhelm their desire to have a potentially good one. As one person put it: "The trip that you do, you like the trip, you will do it again. You get a bad trip, you will think twice before doing it again." Three of our adolescent users "bad-tripped" out of LSD use in this way. After having had many good trips, they had profoundly bad ones, and they never used LSD again.

In summary, there are five factors that may contribute to a bad trip. The two cited most often by the adolescents in their own explanations are a bad underlying mood and bad acid. The worse your mood when you start a trip, or the worse the quality of the acid, the more likely the occurrence of a bad trip. Then there are the personal, situational, and dosage factors that can lead to an intolerable loss of control. As the level of distortion exceeds the youth's personal tolerance level, as the situation introduces factors that must be accurately evaluated and handled, or as the dosage increases toward an intolerable level, the likelihood of a bad trip increases. School LSD trips can be better understood in this light: they are always fairly bad trips because the distortion is too high for effective functioning, but they are rarely profoundly bad because the setting is controlled, benign, and never life threatening.

Advantages and Disadvantages

Tripping experiences were far and away the most important topics for the adolescent users we interviewed. The youths also spent considerable time, however, talking about other attributes of the drug. The positive attributes most often associated with LSD were price, duration of the experience, lack of harmful physical effects, undetectability, and availability. They all agreed that LSD was very readily available.

> [*Interviewer*: So if you and me wanted to go and buy a hit right now, you could just go buy one? It would be pretty easy?]
>
> Oh, yeah. When I was in school, you could get it a lot. It was really easy to get. If you had money, you could get it easy.

All the youths also agreed that LSD is inexpensive, its street price low compared with other illegal drugs. The highest price anyone reported was $5 for one hit. A more common price was $3 per hit, although our interviewees frequently paid less and often got it free from their friends. Most users take from two to four hits in order to produce a trip of approximately five to seven hours' duration. This is a relatively long high when compared with other illegal drugs, making the price of LSD seem even more favorable.

Most of the youths believed that LSD was not physically addictive. Most also recognized that there were no long-term negative physical effects.

> All that I've read has led me to believe that acid does nothing to your body and—I mean, I read books about drugs, lots of books about drugs, and I always first went to the acid section on LSD because I always wanted to know what I was doing to myself. Whenever I smoked PCP or whatever, I would like to know what was happening to me. It was the same over and over again. There have been no proven bad side effects physically. I mean, there have been speculations and whatnot, but I never read a study that indicated that there was a definite problem with LSD use. It was the one drug I found that didn't do anything and it was out of the system in a couple days.

LSD is illegal, so the issue of detectability was important. All the adolescents felt comparatively safe both using and possessing the drug because they believed it to be virtually undetectable. They did not fear drug tests, because there is no simple or convenient test that can establish a person as an LSD user. They all reported that adults appeared unable to recognize a person who was tripping.

> People don't see it. Like when I was on LSD, they thought I was drunk. I got caught like three times while I was on LSD, and every time they said, "What are you, drunk?" I said, "Yeah."

Not only was the trip easy to disguise, but the drug itself was easy to hide.

> I remember I had it laying on my dresser one time—on the paper, had them laying on my dresser on a piece of tin foil one time—and my mom came in and looked at them, and she was like, "Oh, what are these?" I was like, "Oh, it's just a little piece of paper." I was talking on the phone, and I ripped them up, and she was just like, "Oh, okay." That was it, no idea.

> I mean, people get busted for pot and stuff and alcohol in their lockers, but no one really gets busted for acid, ever. It's easy. You can keep it in your wallet, you can keep it anywhere, in a notebook, and behind pages and stuff—it's really easy to keep.

> I know this guy, a cop like pulled him over and he had a sheet of acid in his pocket, like this big, and he didn't want to throw it out the window because they'd see it. He didn't want to have it on his person, he didn't want to have it in his car because he thought they might search in the car, so what he did, he just wrote someone's phone number on it and he crumpled it up and put it in his pocket, and when they checked, they didn't even find it. I mean, it's just so easy to conceal—I mean, it's just so easy. You can put it in the cuff of your sleeve, do anything with it.

LSD, then, carries with it some strategic advantages in comparison to other drugs. But it also has some disadvantages. These include loss of appetite, loss of energy, and sleep disturbances.

> You know, you sit there and you kind of get really tired. That is how I am; I get very, very tired after it like wears off, and I can't sleep because I am so tired. And so do a lot of people I know; they get like that, too.

Such disadvantages are seen as minor on the occasion of any particular trip. But a serious problem can arise with continued heavy use, a problem that—like the profoundly bad trip—can cause a user to quit. This larger problem is actually an accumulation of all the minor problems that, taken singly, were simply viewed as inconveniences. The heavy users (individuals who had tripped at least once a week for years) experienced sleep, diet, and social confusion so great that they became detached from the normal world of their peers. They drifted further and further away from the conventions of everyday life. Their personal and institutional connections simply started to unravel, and the way they dealt with time or their personal appearance became completely disrupted.

> Like one night I'd stay up, I'd go to a party, and the next night I'd stay up and go to a party, then I'd get home at like 3 o'clock, sleep probably till like 1 o'clock the next morning—well, afternoon. I'd wake up and eat some acid, stay awake and just—one day I'd sleep in the night, one day I'd sleep in the afternoon, then the next day I'd sleep in the morning, and just my hours and days were completely just mixed up, you know. That became a problem.

> It came down to personal hygiene, you know—looking good, you know, just going out somewhere, you know. For a jacket, I had a jean jacket with patches all over it; they were all ripped up. I never washed the jacket at all. Jeans that had holes all in them, you know, the ass is sticking out of them. My socks would be just dirty brown, you know; my hair, I'd never comb it. I took a shower probably once or twice a week. I didn't care, didn't care at all, you know—as long as I was on something, I didn't care. It didn't bother me, but I don't know. I mean, it's completely different, you know. I never took time to notice it, you know. Nobody would ever come up to me and say, "Man, you stink." Every once in a while somebody would. I'd just thought they were joking around, you know, I never really noticed it.

The above comment demonstrates one of the more remarkable effects of LSD: it hides from the heavy user its long-term negative effects. The heavy users we talked with had apparently remained unconcerned with, and largely unaware of, the increasing disorganization of their personal lives. They saw the evidence but they simply did not believe it was really happening. Their general impressions were that LSD was creating the illusion that their lives were coming unglued, not that it was causing their lives to come unglued. One of our interviewees explained it this way:

I've never heard anyone say that acid is messing up my life. I've heard them say it about alcohol, pot, PCP, anything else but not acid. 'Cause everybody had it in their head that LSD doesn't have any long-term effects, they could never detect it. [They would say,] "My behavior is still doing fine, it's just that I think it's messed up because of the acid."

I remember one time I had gotten into an argument with my mom, and I had just taken a hit. I was getting ready to go out and it was like an hour after I took the hit, and I was getting ready to leave and my mom asked me something about my jacket or something, and I got really upset with her. I was just like, "Leave me alone, don't you see that I am busy," stuff like that. Then I walk outside with my friends and they would be like, "What was that all about?" And I would be like, "Nothing, I took my hit about an hour ago, that's what it is." And they were like, "Oh, okay." I never really thought twice about it. I kind of thought when I was telling it to my friends that it didn't really happen, that I just thought that it happened and they thought it happened because we were tripping. I thought that it didn't really happen. A lot of people I know have said that.

For the heavy long-term user, the evidence of life disruption finally builds to the point where it can no longer be ignored. Three of our interviewees described how reaching this point caused them to quit taking LSD.

"My life was like all distraught, with relationships with girls, relationships with friends. I was just doing so shitty in school again. I realized that if it went on again like this, I was going to fail, and I didn't want to be stuck in high school like for the rest of my life, so I totally quit."

[*Interviewer*: What made you decide to try to quit? Was it that trip?]

It wasn't, I guess, it wasn't really because of the bad trip. I guess it was because I was tired of doing it so much, you know. I couldn't—I wasn't sleeping at all during the night, I went to school the next day, you know, I'd fall asleep in classes. I was failing a lot of my classes, you know, but I always had a counselor to pull me through so I never failed a grade. My grades were at Ds and Fs, ever since I was in sixth grade. And it's just, you know, I couldn't sleep 'cause I was, you know, eating so much of it. I guess I just got tired of it for a while, take a break from it.

This move to reconnect, then, is the second way that users may spontaneously quit taking LSD. (The first, discussed earlier, is following a very bad trip). A person realizes he or she can't continue to live a disconnected adolescent life forever and therefore stops using LSD.

These two reasons for quitting LSD are related, once again, to the issue of loss of control (the motivation for taking the drug in the first place). When people bad-trip out, they are reacting to having lost control of the trip experience. When people reconnect out of LSD use, they are reacting to cumulative effects that have made them lose control of their lives.

The adolescents see LSD as having certain advantages and disadvantages when compared to other drugs. Among its advantages are availability, low price, a lengthy high, and the ease with which its use can be hidden. Among its disadvantages are loss of sleep and energy and poor diet. Over long periods of heavy use, the disadvantages accumulate into a pattern of disconnection from normal everyday life, a pattern the drug itself leads the youth to consider an illusion. Carried to an extreme, this pattern of disconnection can lead youths to quit using LSD.

Youths and Adults

When the adolescent interviews are contrasted with the two parent interviews and a sample of newspaper articles, interesting differences appear. Some of the differences are so profound that effective communication on the subject of drugs appears almost impossible.

When the parents talk about drugs, they use a system of classification in which drugs are arranged in a hierarchical order: each drug is either more or less bad than other drugs. An underlying assumption holds that use of a drug at one level of "badness" usually leads to use of the drug at the next level. Both parents who were interviewed had trouble understanding LSD, partly because they weren't sure where it fit into the hierarchy.

> A lot of kids are using [LSD]. Is that a step up from marijuana or cocaine?

> If we could keep kids from starting that habit [smoking cigarettes], chances are they are not going to start something worse.

In the parents' system of classification, the defining characteristic of drug is illegality: if a substance was not illegal, it was not considered a drug. Both parents described themselves as people who had never taken drugs. In the course of their interviews, however, they both said that they drank alcohol, and one said she smoked cigarettes and took Valium. None of these substances was considered a real drug because they are not illegal. Illegal drug use, in contrast, was something neither parent could make sense of. This hierarchical typology of illegal drugs, plus the belief that the use of any illegal drug is senseless, hinders the parents' comprehension of the markedly different interpretations used by their children.

The adolescents used a more elaborate system of classification in which any mind-altering substance—not just those deemed illegal—is called a drug. When they spoke of drugs, they included substances like alcohol, butane, and over-the-counter drugs (legal); LSD, marijuana, cocaine, and PCP (illegal); and prescription drugs (semilegal). Not a single adolescent, when talking about LSD or comparing it to other drugs, made reference to a hierarchy of drugs. For the adolescents, each drug has a set of associated negative and positive characteristics, such as the nature and duration of the experience it produces, its availability, and its price. They used this typology when reporting their strategies for drug taking or when comparing two drugs. Legality or illegality was simply one of the characteristics associated with every consciousness-altering substance.

> There was never much physical feeling in it [LSD]; it was all mental, and I think that's how it differs mostly with the NyQuil or Robitussin or whatever you take.

> I knew my parents were starting to get suspicious of me doing drugs, and I have heard that it [LSD] can't show up in tests. And also it was like a fun drug, 'cause like when I smoked marijuana, I get like—eventually I was always getting really tired and I would just sit there and, you know. But like with LSD, it was a fun drug for me because the last time I tripped, I remember I was seeing like little checkerboard things in front of my eyes everywhere.

> Well, in the first place, it's easy to do, man, 'cause you can just pop it in your mouth, you know. It's not like other drugs. Say, reefer, you got to

smoke it, you know, and then, say, cocaine, you gotta smoke it or throw it up in your nose. But see, acid, now you just pop it in your mouth.

Pot gave me more of a mellow sensation, more laid back, kind of set me into a more relaxed mood. Acid, on the other hand, would make things that weren't there appear, and turn things into other things. It would make you more high-strung, like pulsey, more sporadic. It was fast-paced.

Thus there were reasons for taking drugs, and strategies for deciding which ones to take. These strategies made constant reference to the characteristics associated with each drug.

Another contrast between adults and youths centers on the issue of danger. The parents and the newspaper accounts often referred to LSD as dangerous or scary.

It's scary. I am scared more of the thought of LSD than drinking.

You know, these [LSD users] are, believe it or not, people that I have known and that is why it is so scary.

Chemicals going into the brain just scare me.

The adolescent users never referred to the taking of LSD as a dangerous activity. In fact, they seemed to think of LSD as less dangerous than many other drugs because it was undetectable, was not physiologically addictive, and had no harmful physical effects. They did refer to the risks involved in tripping, but they seemed to see these as being manageable through control of the dosage and the situation.

Acid is such an unpredictable drug. I mean, be careful. It doesn't mean anything if somebody is going to be going out and tripping, because anything could happen in their head and they might not have control over it, so watch who you trip with and don't do anything stupid. I mean, don't plan to go to a place where there are going to be a lot of people and drop a lot of acid if you know that you aren't going to want to be there.

For the parents, the danger of LSD centers on the way it produces an unpredictable transformation of the safe, stable life they had established in their community. But it was exactly this transformation that the adolescents were trying to effect.

> "How do kids get to the point where they are self-medicating to the point they are obliterated? You just wonder what these kids are really trying to escape from," said the president of the Parent Teacher Student Association, "Our concern is for the safety of kids and any time you're talking drugs, you're talking about the fact that students are not safe." (Local newspaper)

One parent related this story about her daughter:

> She knew what LSD was. When she was using LSD, I saw her get her old [drug education] notebook out to look up and see what was in it because I was telling her how dangerous it was, and so it really hadn't sunk in, it wasn't enough education. She really didn't know.

The daughter probably hadn't missed the message about danger. She understood what her mother meant about danger, but she attached a different meaning to it. Repeating the warning would not have provided the mother with the desired result, because the dangers of unpredictability and distortion were exactly what the daughter was after.

Danger is a positive part of tripping because it animates what would otherwise be simply a series of interesting illusions. Danger changes an amusing visual show into the adventure that the adolescents seemed to crave. Again and again the adolescents spoke of exploring and journeying while on a trip, and they spoke of LSD adding mystery and giving epic proportions to an experience. On LSD, wandering through the neighborhood park can be a dramatic voyage. By repeatedly emphasizing the dangers of the drug, those in authority make it seem more—rather than less—attractive to youths considering use.

There was also a marked contrast between the way adults and youths described people who take LSD. The parents and newspapers usually characterized LSD users as being bad, in trouble, and often not local residents.

> They were troublemakers that had been in trouble repeatedly, and I think [my daughter] first encountered them outside the teen center

here. Now these kids aren't allowed in, but it's hard to keep them from hanging around outside. I do know that there is a roving group that is dangerous, and I do know that some of these kids have parents who protect them from the police. They need help. These are obviously not normal kids.

It was a group of kids who are much more notorious than the ones that live here, that travel through areas, and on their way through areas they will pick up kids that could be easily attracted to them. The children that I noticed, that were foulmouthed and would wait on the cul-de-sac instead of coming into the door, were kids that didn't really go to [the local school] but were going to school in [another county]. They talked a lot of our kids into taking LSD.

The adolescents painted an entirely different picture of the type of people who were using LSD.

At my school the cheerleaders do it, some people on the football team do it. Some preps do it, some headbangers do it. There is just not really anybody, it's everybody.

There have been people that I found out that had done acid that I had no idea of. I mean, it's just a basic thing at my school—almost everybody that I could think of has done it and a lot of them are still doing it, and I know it's that way in a lot of other schools. There is just a lot of people doing it.

There are a lot of people doing it. It's not just limited to certain cliques. I know jocks that do it, just everybody. You can find, in every little social group, you're going to find people that do acid. Preps, jocks, everybody. It's everywhere.

The adults characterized a habitual drug user as being an evil or troubled person. Because they did not see their own children or their children's friends as either of these things, they also tended to characterize the "real" users as different from their children. The real users were "those other kids," usually from somewhere else. By connecting drug users and "troubled youths," the adults linked drug problems with such social problems as street crime, gangs, fractured family structure, and poverty. The way they coded the drug problem made it something they expected in the inner city, not in a stable, upper-middle-class suburban community. The existence of a drug problem and their vision of their community were as incompatible as their image of a drug user and their vision of their children.

> "It's shocking and new to us," said the president of the Parent Teacher Student Association. "I'm personally appalled this is going on. It's made us all stop and think. It does threaten your sense of security. Some people moved to the suburbs, and that's their safety net. This [LSD use] is a wake-up call that it's not safe." (Local newspaper)

The irony here is that the suburban community provides both the motivation for LSD use and the protected setting in which to use it. The adolescents we talked with wanted to have adventures through which they could test themselves against the world. They all believed that their suburban community made these adventures impossible. It was the safety, predictability, and homogeneity of their suburban neighborhood that they said they were trying to escape. LSD provided this escape by creating novelty and unpredictability.

> Down here, man, I have nothing to do. That's what I think why people do drugs, because there's nothing to do. This state is like the boonies, man, there ain't anything to do. See, you're going to sit home and, you know, I think people in this county is getting more acid because people just want out. They want to have fun.

> I can think of a thousand things I would like to be doing.
>   [*Interviewer*: Why don't you just do them?]
>   Because they won't let me out of high school. High school is like a prison.

> It sucks, it's terribly boring. It's why a lot of people do acid. There's nothing to do around here. It really sucks, I mean I live in [name of town], and it's just really boring. The only thing there really is to do is go to the movies, or maybe go downtown and get drunk or something, you know. It's like people drink, people drive for fun, because it's a change. Even like sitting in a room, it's totally boring, but you can like take acid, smoke, do any sorta drug and being in the room will be like exciting, you know. That's why a lot of people do drugs, you know. Because they don't want to be bored.

The predictability and safety of the suburban community also provide the perfect setting in which to take LSD. The private and comfortable basement bedroom, the shopping mall, or the suburban park exemplify the safe setting in which a good trip is more likely to occur. LSD thus fits perfectly into the suburban setting. It transforms a predictable setting into an adventure, but it requires that predictable setting to produce a good trip.

The differences between adults and the adolescent users are evident when they talk about the motivation for LSD use. Because taking any drug was seen by the parents as senseless, they had trouble finding a reason for their children's LSD use. They believed that kids first tried LSD because of coercion, and that after the kids were hooked, their continued use of LSD was motivated by social pressure.

This explanation of motive fit with the rest of their model of use. Coercion was the kind of behavior you would expect from "those bad kids from over there"; and only social pressure would keep a youth doing something as senseless as taking LSD. The model of the predatory habitual user was coded into their name for the people who sold drugs. The parents often called these people *drug pushers,* implying that the sellers didn't respond to any desire to buy but instead pushed the drugs on their customers.

> My daughter said the kids who buy it ask to buy it, and they are not co-erced. Of course they are. I said that from the minute you meet these kids, they are warming up to get you to buy it. Just because they pretend to be your friend first doesn't mean that they aren't dangerous.

> I would like to try to paint people who sell drugs as dirty and conniving and pretending to be your friend so that they could get into your pocket, even if that means that they have to take you out and talk to you and spend time with you and pretend to be a friend and really betray you. They will get you in this habit for the money, for what you've got in your purse or your pocket.

These comments by the parents contrast strongly with those of the adolescents, most of whom reported that they first tried LSD out of curiosity to see what the experience was like:

> I'd heard about it, you know. I wasn't peer-pressured into it, I wasn't— I mean, a lot of people don't believe that, but I went up to someone because I'd heard so much about it, and I wanted to try it.

When the adolescents described their patterns of LSD use, they varied greatly among individuals. But these patterns were not haphazard or unplanned, nor were they shaped by social coercion. The adolescents reported a clear idea of their objectives, and they controlled the time, amount, and mixing of the drugs they took. The strategies they employed took account of the positive and negative attributes they associated with LSD.

I mean, I had found it in ninth grade, but when I realized the potential when you dropped a little bit more I was amazed—I was really amazed. So I just started dropping more and more at a time. In general, I dropped not very much more than once a week because with a trip on Sunday and then a trip on Wednesday, you don't trip very well on Wednesday. So I liked to get as much out of it as I could, so I'd wait like six or seven days in between trips. An average, I guess, would be once a week.

I was getting to the point where I was doing two, three, four hits—three or four mostly. When I was doing that much, I didn't sleep, I wasn't eating as much. I couldn't eat when I tripped because food did not look appetizing. I didn't take care of myself real well, then I cut down and then everything would get back into swing, or I would stop for a while. When I got like that, when I wasn't taking care of myself, I'd stop for a few weeks, then I would start up again.

Sometimes, most of the time, it was just acid that we would use. If we were going to do acid it was just acid because, you know, we heard all sorts of things—if you do acid and you drink, then the alcohol takes away from the trip. So I know that is still going around. A lot of people still say that. A lot of people don't drink when they are tripping. We did once in a while. Sometimes we smoked pot when we did acid. It wasn't that often; most of the times we did acid, it was just acid, that's all.

Well, you know when you feel like doing it, because if you do it too much, you get real sweaty and you feel real blah all the time, yucky, and you break out. So a lot of people just don't like that, so they only do it sometimes. Like my crowd, we don't trip all the time. It's like once a month or maybe twice; no, not even, yeah, once a month. Maybe sometimes it's like every day, but when it's once a month then you take three, and that is a lot. When it's almost every day, you take one—you have to stop 'cause if you take acid one hit one day, then you have to take two the next, then three the next day. That is why we don't do it, because we just like to take one or two or three. So you know, we take three and then wait like a week or two, take another three, so we get that high.

The strategies, as we've seen, don't always work; the reactions by some of the interviewees to profoundly bad trips and the long-term effect of disconnection from ordinary life make that case. But the point here is that the youths all reported that they sought out and managed the LSD experience, rather than having been coerced into a senseless act, as the adults viewed the situation.

In summary, adults and LSD-using youths offer quite different views of LSD. Adults consider drugs to be illegal substances that can be arranged in a hierarchy of badness. They see LSD as danger-ous—as a disruption of the ordered, secure world they desire for themselves and their children. Users are a particular type of child, problem kids who typically come from outside the community. Use itself is senseless, irrational, something that any reasonable youth would do only if forced.

The youths, in contrast, see legal and illegal drugs as an array of different kinds of experiences, each with its advantages and disad-vantages. The immediate danger of LSD is that it is illegal; other-wise, the disruption of order and predictability—the danger the adults see—is one of the results that the youths seek. Many differ-ent kinds of youths use LSD; its use is not confined to any one so-cial group. Instead, youths seek particular effects from LSD, and they attempt to manage their use to control those effects.

Conclusion

LSD is a drug that young people take because they enjoy the expe-rience it produces. It transforms the elements of conventional life into an amazing, unpredictable, and interesting adventure. It does this by distorting the user's cognitive processes: during a trip, per-ception, reasoning, and memory all operate in new and unpre-dictable ways.

The answer to the question "Why do youths use LSD?" lies in the nature of the experience. A good trip is fun, makes the world more interesting, and makes the user more creative; it forges social bonds, excludes adults, and unfolds in settings that users find pleasant and safe.

Use can sometimes turn problematic, however, in one of two ways. First, bad trips occur because of poor mood or drug quality, or because the situation, the personal limits on how much distortion a user can tolerate, or the dose level take the trip beyond the user's control. While some bad trips are expected as part of the game, others can turn profoundly terrifying. Severely unpleasant trips are one of the major reasons youths quit using LSD.

Second, although LSD is cheap and safe compared to other illegal drugs, its disadvantages (such as problems with sleep and diet) can turn problematic with long-term heavy use. Users may become so detached from normal life—and so blind to the problem, because it is considered just another illusion—that they cease to function in their worlds. Such disconnection is a second major reason youths quit using the drug.

The adults' view of LSD, as noted in the previous section, contrasts sharply with the youths' view. For the adults, LSD is illegal and ranks high on the scale of drug problems. Its use is dangerous and senseless, something that their children were coerced into. For the youths, LSD is a distinct substance among many others (legal and illegal) with particular effects that they seek out and try to manage, and it is something used by many types of adolescents.

Epidemiologic surveys have shown that the most frequent user of LSD in the 1990s is a white middle- or upper-middle-class adolescent. Based on the analysis above, we can hazard some guesses about why this is the case. The drug is inexpensive and generally easy to find, making it in principle available to everyone. It transforms the ordinary into the extraordinary and unpredictable, so it would be favored by youths for whom boredom is a major fact of life and avoided by those who feel their lives are already too challenging and unpredictable. It makes the user feel powerless and unable to cope with difficult situations, so it would be favored by individuals who can assume benign and safe worlds to which they can return after tripping. It temporarily impairs the user's judgment, so it requires a comparatively safe and dependable location for use. The heavy user becomes increasingly irresponsible and unproductive; this suggests a person with few responsibilities who is part of a community that has the strength, resilience, and resources to continue supporting him or her as a noncontributing member.

This model explains the statistical association of LSD use and white, relatively affluent adolescents in terms of the world of middle-class suburbia—a world that is predominantly white, relatively affluent, and provides relative safety. An urban world, one where unpredictability and danger abound, where a person needs to maintain control and where poverty offers little support, suggests a poor fit with LSD. In fact, the one inner-city Hispanic interviewee described just such a world, and he was the only one of our adolescent participants who seldom used the drug.

LSD may be the drug of affluent discontent. Affluence provides the base that makes use possible, and discontent with the order and stability often accompanying that affluence provides the motive. Such a conclusion is surely too simple, but it corresponds with the epidemiologic facts and, we hope, suggests further questions to deepen our outsiders' understanding of why youths use LSD.

It is important to note that this analysis was built on six interviews with former LSD users in treatment. For this reason, the study is a report from a segment of the world of heavy involvement with the drug. A more comprehensive understanding of youths and LSD would require more work, interviews, and participant observation, with a broader range of youths as well as a richer understanding of the texture of their worlds. We hope that such a work will soon be conducted.

2

About LSD

Leigh A. Henderson

Hallucinogens

LSD is a member of the class of drugs called hallucinogens. Hallucinogens are chemical compounds that alter sensory perception, thought, and feeling. They occur naturally in a wide range of plants, including the peyote cactus and the psilocybin mushroom. Hallucinogens have been used among various peoples for centuries and perhaps millennia, often in sacred rituals.

Many terms have been coined to describe the effects of these drugs. These include *psychotomimetic* (psychosis-mimicking), *psychotogenic* (psychosis-causing), *psycholytic* (mind-loosening), *psychodysleptic* (mind-disrupting), *psychedelic* (mind-revealing), *phanerothyme* (soul-revealing), *mysticomimetic, emotionalgenic, mind-expanding, consciousness-expanding, transcendental, illusogenic, phantasticant*, and *deliriant*.

The term *hallucinogen* is itself something of a misnomer. True hallucinations occur when a person sees or hears something that does not exist, and believes that what is seen or heard is real. The hallucinations produced by hallucinogenic drugs are different: they are usually visual, resulting when information about what the eye sees is distorted on its way to the brain. In short, persons on hallucinogenic drugs see what we see, but they perceive it differently. And most of the time, they are aware that what they perceive—

things like faces melting, or letters running off the end of a printed page—is caused by the drug.

There are several different systems of classification for hallucinogenic drugs. In terms of chemical structure, they have been classified into five groups. Three of these are commonly found in the street drug market: lysergic acid amines (LSD), phenylalkylamines (peyote and mescaline), and indolealkylamines (psilocybin). The effects of these drugs are similar. In fact, LSD is often sold as mescaline or sprayed on common mushrooms and sold as psilocybin mushrooms. The Drug Enforcement Administration (DEA), meanwhile, classifies all drugs according to the 1970 Comprehensive Drug Abuse Prevention and Control Act. All psychoactive drugs are divided into five classes based on abuse potential, current accepted medical use, and safety. Lysergic acid amides, phenylalkylamines, and indolealkylamines were placed under Schedule I (high abuse potential, no current medical use, and a lack of safety for use under medical supervision). Legal penalties are highest for this group of drugs, which includes heroin and other narcotics.

Surveys on drug use often expand the category of hallucinogens to include phencyclidine (PCP) and "ecstasy" (3,4-methylenedioxymethamphetamine, or MDMA). These drugs affect the central nervous system very differently from LSD, mescaline, and psilocybin; the use of PCP, in particular, can have very serious consequences. Statistics that combine these groups under the rubric of "hallucinogen users" therefore conceal important information. For example, many surveys fail to distinguish between LSD and PCP, the two most common hallucinogens, yet PCP and LSD are used by different populations. PCP users are usually black males between twenty and thirty-nine years of age, while LSD users are most frequently white males below the age of thirty.

Background

LSD was first synthesized in 1938 by Albert Hofmann, a chemist at the Sandoz pharmaceutical laboratories in Basel, Switzerland.˙ The

---

˙Hofmann eventually was appointed head of the Pharmaceutical-Chemical Research Laboratories for Sandoz, Ltd.

work was part of a systematic investigation into the properties of ergot (a rye grass fungus) as a source of new medicines. Several successful products were developed during this research, including drugs to induce labor in pregnant women, to improve blood circulation and brain function in the elderly, and to stabilize blood pressure.

Lysergic acid diethylamide (in German, *Lysergsäure-diäthylamid*) was the twenty-fifth in a series of lysergic acid derivatives. For laboratory use, the name was abbreviated to LSD-25.* LSD-25 was specifically created with the idea that it might be a circulatory and respiratory stimulant. Tests showed that it stimulated contraction of the uterus, although not as strongly as other drugs. Sandoz pharmacologists and physicians found nothing exceptional in these properties, though, and testing of LSD-25 was abandoned.

Hofmann remained interested in the drug, and in 1943 synthesized a new batch of LSD-25. That afternoon, he experienced two hours of an unusual intoxication: he felt restless and slightly dizzy, his imagination was active, and he "perceived an uninterrupted stream of fantastic pictures, extraordinary shapes with intense, kaleidoscopic play of colors."[12] Hofmann later speculated that he must have absorbed a minute amount through his skin[†] and concluded that LSD-25 was extraordinary potent.

Hofmann decided to experiment further. Cautiously, he took a 250-microgram oral dose of LSD;[††] if LSD-25 were similar to other ergot alkaloids, a smaller amount would have no effect. (Later experiments would show that 30 to 50 micrograms was an effective dose.) Hofmann described the surprisingly powerful experience:

> The following were the most outstanding symptoms: vertigo; visual disturbances; the faces of those around me appeared as grotesque, colored masks; marked motoric unrest, alternating with paralysis; an intermittent heavy feeling in the head, limbs and the entire body . . . ; dry, constricted sensation in the throat; feeling of choking; clear recognition of my condition, in which state I observed . . . that I shouted half

---

*The *Dictionary of American Slang* (London: George G. Harrap & Co., Ltd., 1967) suggests erroneously that LSD-25 was so named because it was created on the second day of the fifth month.

[†]LSD is in fact not absorbed through skin; Hofmann most likely touched his LSD-contaminated fingers to his mouth.

[††]1 microgram = 1 millionth of a gram (10^{-6}).

insanely or babbled incoherent words. Occasionally I felt as if I were out of my body.

Six hours after ingestion of the LSD, my condition had already improved considerably. Only the visual disturbances were still pronounced. . . . A remarkable feature was the manner in which all acoustic perceptions . . . were transformed into optical effects. . . . I . . . awoke next morning feeling perfectly well.[13]

The symptoms Hofmann describes are typical of an LSD experience, or trip. Other researchers at Sandoz were able to replicate Hofmann's experiences using doses one-third as large.

LSD-25 had several unusual properties that promised to be of significance in pharmacology, neurology, and psychiatry. After safety testing on animals, systematic human experiments were carried out using doses of LSD ranging from 20 to 130 micrograms.[14] LSD-25 had a profound psychoactive effect at a very low dose. Subjects remained aware that the experience was drug induced, and they could later recall some or most of what was experienced while under the influence of the drug. There was little residual effect or hangover. Sandoz introduced LSD-25 to European research institutions in 1947, marketing it in 25-microgram tablets and 100-microgram ampoules. The prospectus recommended that LSD be used in analytical psychotherapy "to elicit release of repressed material and provide mental relaxation," and in experimental studies on psychoses. It stated that LSD would induce "model psychoses of short duration in normal subjects." Sandoz recommended that psychiatrists take LSD themselves "to gain an insight into the world of ideas and sensations of mental patients."[12] The drug was supplied free of charge to experimental and clinical investigators.

LSD was introduced to the United States in 1949 at the Boston Psychopathic Hospital; the first recommendation of the use of LSD as an adjunct to psychotherapy was published in 1950.[15] Its use spread initially in the psychiatric and scientific communities. A symposium on psychedelic drugs was held at the annual meeting of the American Psychiatric Association in 1953.* An international conference devoted to LSD was held in 1959, and by 1960 there were more than five hundred scientific papers on LSD in print. Altogether, some one hundred scientific reports on LSD were published every year from 1956 through the mid-1960s.[16] In 1965, over two hundred research studies using LSD and other hallucinogens in human subjects were in progress.[17]

In the early 1950s, the Central Intelligence Agency (CIA) became interested in LSD's potential as a "truth drug" or mind control agent.[18] In the CIA's cold-war "Operation MK-ULTRA," experiments were conducted using numerous mind-altering drugs (as well as parapsychology). Because minute amounts of it were so powerful, LSD was a focal point. By the mid-1960s, some one thousand five hundred military personnel had received LSD (not always knowingly) in experiments conducted by the Army Chemical Corps. In 1977, this highly classified program was investigated by the Senate Subcommittee on Health and Scientific Research. It became apparent that the scientific merit of many of the studies was questionable, the use of unknowing subjects was unethical and perhaps illegal, and that self-experimentation among the investigators was rampant.

As the psychedelic properties of LSD became known outside the psychiatric community, the nonmedical use of LSD spread. It was available on the black market at least as early as 1962,[19] and it became a central part of the social and cultural youth rebellion of the 1960s. The role played by LSD and other psychedelic drugs in this period of American history has received extensive attention.[16, 18, 20–23]

LSD was readily available for clinical and experimental research until 1963, when the last of the Sandoz patents expired. In that same year the U.S. Food and Drug Administration amended the Federal Food, Drug, and Cosmetics Act of 1938 to classify LSD as an "investigational new drug" (IND), restricted to use by researchers on federal and state grants. Researchers who retained stocks of LSD had to turn them over to the government by 1965. Sandoz stopped production and distribution of LSD and other hallucinogens in 1966, citing widespread misconceptions about LSD and concern over lack of regulation;[12, 16] its stockpile of LSD was turned over to the National Institute of Mental Health.[24] A United Nations committee called for worldwide regulatory action on LSD.[25]

'The symposium was addressed by Aldous Huxley. Huxley was an early advocate of the carefully planned nonmedical use of hallucinogens as a means to a higher consciousness.

The first federal criminal sanctions against LSD were introduced in the Drug Abuse Control Amendments of 1965. Unlawful manufacture of amphetamines, barbiturates, and hallucinogens became a misdemeanor; possession carried no penalty. These amendments were modified in 1968: possession became a misdemeanor, and sale a felony. Individual states determined penalties, although most adopted the federal classification system.

Some seventy research projects on LSD were in progress in 1966, despite increased regulation of experimental use. The approval process for research involving hallucinogenic drugs, however, had become restrictive. The government was reluctant to fund projects involving LSD, and by 1969, only a half-dozen such studies existed.[26] The last National Institute of Mental Health (NIMH) projects using LSD in human subjects ended in 1974. In 1980 only one clinical IND project was active; it explored the use of LSD in terminally ill cancer patients.[27, 28]

In the 1990s research into any of the hallucinogens using human beings is almost nonexistent, and the process of obtaining permission remains extremely difficult.[29] Pharmacologic research in animals has continued, however, and nonhallucinogenic derivatives of LSD have proven extremely useful in studies of serotonin receptors.[30-37]

Pharmacology

LSD affects the central nervous system at multiple sites, and thus it has multiple effects.[38] The molecular structure of LSD is similar to that of the neurotransmitter serotonin. LSD therefore has a high affinity for serotonin receptors and interferes with the normal functioning of these receptors. An association between brain serotonin and the action of LSD was proposed as early as 1954,[39] and serotonin receptors have been confirmed as the major sites of action of LSD. Serotonin has a significant role in sensory perception and control of mood;[40] however, the exact mechanism that produces LSD's unique effects is still not understood.[41] Researchers are now attempting to identify the serotonin receptor subtypes that are affected, and to determine whether LSD inhibits or stimulates neurotransmission.[42-47] Recent research suggests that it can do both, and that its effects may vary at different locations in the brain.

LSD also affects the visual pathways.[48–50] LSD appears to affect visual processing in the retina, as well as interfere with the electrical conduction of visual information to the brain. In a comparison of the effects of LSD in blind and sighted humans,[51] similar levels of electrical activity occurred in the retina in both groups. Blind subjects who could once see, and whose optic nerves retained some function, could perceive hallucinations. Hallucinations could occur in persons with abnormal retinas, but did not occur if the optic nerves had atrophied.

LSD is easily absorbed through the gastrointestinal tract. It is metabolized in the liver, and its metabolites are excreted in bile through the small intestine; only about 1 percent is excreted unaltered in the urine.[52, 53] If a person consumes 1 microgram of LSD per kilo of body weight, half of the drug will have been metabolized in about five hours (its half-life).[54] In comparison, heroin and cocaine are metabolized much more quickly; their half-lives are thirty and fifty minutes, respectively.[38, 55] Marijuana persists in the blood much longer than LSD; its half-life is some thirty hours.[38]

As little as 0.25 micrograms of LSD per kilo of body weight (17.5 micrograms for a person weighing 155 pounds) can produce mild physical effects. Doses of 1 or 2 micrograms/kilo (70–140 micrograms for a 155-pound person) produce LSD's characteristic perceptual and psychic effects.[39] LSD's most profound psychic effect, the sense of contacting some profound universal truth, occurs at higher doses. The dosage common in the early 1960s, (when achieving this cosmic consciousness was often a motivation for LSD use) was 250 micrograms; in the 1990s the common dosage is believed to be 50 micrograms.

Tolerance to LSD (meaning that the body adjusts to repeated doses of the drug, and no longer experiences its physical or mental effects) develops quickly. In an early experiment, tolerance developed after three days of daily administration of LSD.[39] Once tolerance was developed, administration of as much as four times the standard dose of LSD had no effect. Tolerance was lost, though, as quickly as it developed.

A toxicity level for LSD in humans has not been established, but the risk of death from an overdose of LSD is virtually nonexistent. The standard laboratory measurement of toxicity is the LD_{50}—the lethal dose at which half the experimental animals die. For LSD, the LD_{50} is inversely related to the size of the animal; thus for mice, rats, and rabbits, the LD_{50} for LSD injected intravenously is 46, 16.5, and 0.3 milligrams/kilo (mg/k), respectively.[56] An elephant was killed by the injection of 0.1 mg/k.[57] From these data, the LD_{50} for humans has been estimated at 0.2 mg/k injected intravenously, or 14,000 micrograms in a 155-pound person.[52] To consume this much LSD, it would be necessary to swallow 56 of the 250-microgram tablets available in the 1960s, or 280 of the 50-microgram doses commonly available in the 1990s. In fact, a lethal dose might be much higher, because the estimate is based on injecting rather than swallowing LSD.

The medical literature contains two reports of deaths attributed to an LSD overdose; for neither of these cases, though, are the full circumstances of the death available. In the first, a thirty-four-year-old was found dead in a deserted warehouse.[58] He had last been seen a month earlier, engaged in bizarre behavior and attempting to break into a building. A high level of LSD (and no other drugs or alcohol) was found in his liver. As no other cause of death was apparent, it was concluded that the man might have died from LSD-induced respiratory arrest. In the second case, a twenty-five-year-old man died sixteen hours after being admitted to a hospital.[59] High levels of LSD were found in his liver, blood, and stomach contents. Tests for amphetamines and cannabinoids were negative, but it is not stated whether tests were made for other drugs or for alcohol.

Clinical Effects

LSD's effects begin to be noticeable some thirty minutes to an hour after ingestion, peak two to five hours later, and may continue for eight to twelve hours or more. Both physical and psychic effects vary from person to person. The duration and intensity of the experience is highly dependent on the dose; an increased dosage will prolong the effects of LSD.[39, 60]

Physical effects appear first. Dilated pupils (mydriasis) and increased deep tendon reflexes (hyperreflexia) are the only consistent neurologic changes.[39] Blood pressure is usually elevated, and body temperature may be normal[39] or slightly elevated.[61] Other perceptible effects may include increased heart rate (tachycardia), blurred vision, nausea, gooseflesh (piloerection), weakness, tingling in the fingers and toes (paresthesia), dizziness, sweating, and tremors.[38] Drowsiness is sometimes cited as an effect, although LSD more often seems to keep the user awake. Appetite is reported to decrease, although it might be more accurate to say that interest in food is lessened. LSD does not effect brain circulation, liver function, or cholesterol, although blood sugar may be elevated.[52]

Sensory-perceptual changes are the outstanding features of an LSD experience. As noted before, LSD does not produce true hallucinations; true hallucinations are experienced without sensory cues, and the subject believes in the reality of the perception. LSD alters the way in which existing sensory stimuli are perceived, and the user typically remains aware that his or her perceptions are drug induced.[62-63]

Visual disturbances are characteristic of LSD. The types of disturbance reported are remarkably consistent over time and across subjects. Images may be perceived with eyes open or closed. Geometric shapes are common, as is the perception of images or figures in patterns. Flashes of color occur, and color is generally intensified. Stable objects may seem to move, usually in the peripheral vision. Objects may have halos. Afterimages can cause trailing phenomena, in which images remain as an object moves across the visual field (rather like the frames of a motion picture). Objects may appear to be larger or smaller than they actually are. Hallucinations of the other senses—hearing, taste, and smell—are rare. Other sensory/perceptual changes include an overall heightened sense of beauty; sounds/or textures (like colors) may become more intense. Time can be grossly distorted; it may seem to slow, to speed up, or even to run backward.

One of the most interesting phenomena associated with LSD is cross-sensory perception, or *synesthesia*. Synesthesia is defined medically as a condition in which a stimulus causes a sensation beyond what is usual and normal.[64] The most common form is "colored hearing," in which music, voices, or other noises evoke perceptions of specific colors and shapes.[65-67] Other combinations of senses have also been described. Although natural occurrence of this phenomenon is rare, it has been recognized for at least two hundred years.

Euphoria is often the first reaction to LSD; users grin, giggle, or laugh. A person on LSD is emotionally suggestible; feelings are intensified and may change abruptly in response to changes in the setting. Over the course of the trip, users' emotions change rapidly; paranoia and hostility may develop, then be followed by periods of calm or excitement. Occasionally psychotic states characterized by extreme anxiety develop, but these are usually limited to the period of intoxication.[68] The LSD experience is greatly dependent on the setting, the emotional state and background of the user, and the expectations for the experience.

A feeling of detachment from one's body often develops. This has been variously called depersonalization, dissociation, derealization, body image distortion, and even levitation.[69-71] This feeling that one's body is not one's own, or that one is standing beside oneself, may hamper physical coordination. Users may temporarily lose their sense of identity, but they are usually not delirious.[69] Thoughts are dreamlike, flowing freely; short-term memory and abstract reasoning are impaired, as are judgment and impulse control. The user generally compensates for these effects, however, by withdrawal and a low level of activity.[72]

To an observer, a person on LSD may appear to be frighteningly incoherent. Users may have trouble expressing themselves, or they may speak in bursts containing flights of ideas, separated by long pauses. They may also appear to have short attention spans. Part of the difficulty in expression is the nature of the LSD experience itself. A person is inclined to turn inward; communication with someone not sharing the experience is not important. The attention span for tasks or conversation is short because the user is more interested in the LSD trip. However, a person on LSD may concentrate for long periods on something small, such as the palm of his or her hand. Finally, LSD users are often incoherent because so much of the experience is indescribable; words cannot adequately convey it.

At doses of about 3 micrograms/kilo body weight (210 micrograms for a 155-pound man), many users report a transpersonal state of consciousness. It is often described as feeling that the mind is transcending the boundaries of the individual self; space, time, and identity are all disarranged. The user may interpret this as a religious, mystical, or metaphysical experience. LSD users who have this kind of experience carry a recollection of it as strange, awesome, and beautiful, often yielding a profound knowledge of oneself.[69]

Objective tests of perceptual, psychomotor, and cognitive functioning while users are under the influence of LSD are difficult to carry out and to interpret. The effect of the drug is so distinctive that placebo-controlled trials cannot be conducted. The subject will always know whether he or she has received LSD, as will the researcher. Because of this the clinical setting, the testing methods, and the understanding and expectations of the researcher will inevitably influence the nature of the experience.[17] Abnormal responses may only mean that the subject, intensely absorbed in his experience, is unwilling to carry out the investigator's request. The often-conflicting results of scientists who have tried to measure altered subjective perceptions may be attributable in part to such problems.

Therapeutic Use

LSD was greeted as a wonder drug by the psychiatric profession. Penicillin, introduced only a few years earlier in 1943, was effecting almost overnight cures in previously untreatable diseases like syphilis and pneumonia. It seems in retrospect that LSD was expected to do the same for mental disease: the powerful paranormal (or mystical, transcendental, or visionary—no single term seems accurate) experience of LSD, guided by a therapist, would effect near-miraculous personality changes. Psychiatrists wrote of "spectacular and almost unbelievable results" and "instantaneous transformations."[73] At least one envisioned "mass therapy: institutions in which every patient with a neurosis could get LSD treatment and work out his problems largely by himself."[74] More prosaically, LSD was expected to shorten the lengthy and expensive process of psychotherapy; it would enable patients to recall the childhood experiences and unconscious material that often did not emerge for months or years in conventional psychotherapy. LSD was a drug that would effect fundamental changes in attitudes and personality, not just a reduction in the outward symptoms of mental illness. It was expected to be of particular value in patients who were resistant to more conventional therapies.

LSD was used in the treatment of an enormous range of neurotic and psychotic states. These included schizophrenia in adults and children, childhood autism, obsessive-compulsive symptoms,

Tourette's syndrome, anxiety, anorexia, and phantom limb pain.[75-87] Sexual "perversions" ranging from homosexuality to impotence, masochism, exhibitionism, and transvestitism were treated with LSD.[83, 88-92] Attempts were made to reform criminals through the use of LSD therapy.[92] There was also interest in using LSD to help terminally ill patients confront and accept death.[28, 93-95]

Between 1950 and the mid-1960s, psychedelic drug therapy generated more than one thousand clinical papers discussing 40,000 patients, as well as six international conferences and several dozen books.[16] Two principal theoretical schools for the use of LSD in psychotherapy were developed; in each, LSD was used as a tool to stimulate recall of early experiences and as a way to discover the subconscious.[23, 96] Psycholytic therapy was practiced mainly in Europe and used a series of low-dose (50 micrograms) LSD sessions to encourage memories of childhood, to explore subconscious symbolism, and to shorten therapy. Psychedelic therapy, more common in the United States, used one or two high-dose (usually 200 to 250 milligrams) LSD sessions in the hope that a transcendent experience would encourage the patient to reshape his or her life. The subject would then become less depressed, anxious, guilty, or angry, and more self-tolerant, religious, and sensually aware.[16, 96]

A full review of the mass of research on LSD therapy is beyond the scope of this book. Evaluation of much of this research is difficult: many studies involved only a few people, and before about 1970 most researchers did not compare results in patients treated with LSD to results in an untreated group. Thus many of the patients who improved (or grew worse) might have done so *without* LSD therapy: they may have recovered spontaneously or as a result of other components of the treatment.

Perhaps the greatest hopes for LSD were pinned on its use in treating alcoholism, which has proved resistant to traditional therapies. At first psychiatrists hoped that LSD would cause a "model delirium tremens," essentially frightening the alcoholic into reforming.[52, 97] The treatment concept that evolved is more like the self-help programs that are central in treating alcohol and other drug addiction today, entailing a spiritual reawakening of the addict (variously called "hitting bottom," "surrendering," or "admitting powerlessness"). It was believed that LSD could create this kind of peak experience, generating a profound sense of meaning and intense positive emotion that would lead to a cure. Early studies showed apparent success, but they were later shown to be flawed—either there were no untreated patients for comparison, the researchers knew which patients had been given LSD, or the measures of success were not defined.[98] Later studies that included groups for comparison could show no lasting positive effect of LSD in treating alcoholics.[99]

LSD therapy in terminal illness remained the last use approved by the federal government, and research continued into the 1980s. This therapy also relied on the peak experience and was supplemented by intensive psychologic preparation of the patient and his or her family. The goal of LSD therapy was to help the patient remain alert and aware while providing relief from pain and discomfort. It was meant to lessen the sense of isolation, and to help the patient reach out to those close to him or her.[28] The therapeutic use of LSD in the terminally ill had some success in studies without comparison groups, but it has not been widely explored.[28, 96] The preparation of the patient and family before giving the LSD may have contributed to its apparent success.

Disappointment in the initially promising future of LSD was expressed as early as 1968, when at least two published papers proclaimed a consensus that LSD therapy could help only a few carefully selected and treated patients.[100, 101] The 1974 NIMH Research Task Force declared there was no therapeutic use for LSD.[102] Interest in hallucinogenic drugs as aids to psychotherapy is still alive, however, and drugs that produce the fantasies and insights of LSD without its perceptual and mood changes are seen as potentially valuable to psychiatry.[17, 29, 96, 103–106] Many researchers feel that hallucinogenic drug research was prematurely arrested.

Manufacturing and Marketing

LSD used outside the scientific community was at first produced by Sandoz and diverted to the black market. LSD was manufactured illicitly as early as 1962[24] and in quantity after 1966, when Sandoz stopped production of its hallucinogens. Wholesale production is believed to have been based in northern California, primarily in the San Francisco area, for some twenty-five years. The DEA, however, reports that an increasing number of independent entrepreneurs are manufacturing LSD. Laboratories operating at least sporadically have been identified in Denver, Boulder, Hartford, New Orleans, and Austin.[107]

LSD is an attractive product for illegal manufacture because it is so potent. An amount as small as 10 micrograms can produce a mild euphoria and loosening of inhibitions. One kilo of pure LSD is equal to 20 million dosage units (using the DEA's standard dosage unit of 50 micrograms) and a batch of 25 to 100 grams (0.5 to 2 million dosage units) can be made in two or three days.[107]

The manufacture of LSD requires skill, good equipment, and access to the precursor chemicals. Although LSD itself is classified as Schedule I under the Controlled Substances Act, the chemicals used in its manufacture are less restricted. Lysergic acid and lysergic acid amide, for example, are classified as Schedule III (some abuse potential). Ergotamine tartrate and ergonovine, although not manufactured in the United States, have legitimate medical uses and are classified as Schedule V (low abuse potential). It is estimated that about 4 kilograms of ergotamine tartrate can produce 1 kilogram of LSD. Other essential chemicals are readily available and also have legitimate uses.[107]

Pure crystalline LSD is converted to powder or dissolved in water. It is then made into ingestible forms and packaged in individual doses at conversion laboratories. These forms have included tablets ("microdot"), squares of gelatin ("windowpane"), and capsules. A drop of liquid LSD is sometimes put on a sugar cube, an aspirin, or a breath mint. The most common form of LSD in the United States is "blotter acid," in which sheets of absorbent paper are dipped in a solution of LSD tartrate dissolved in methanol or ethanol. The sheets of paper, roughly the size of a dollar bill, are usually preprinted with cartoon characters or emblems such as stars, planets, mystical symbols, or musical notes.[108, 109, *]

---

*A persistent myth is the "Blue Star tattoo" legend, which for more than a dozen years has circulated in communities in the United States and England. Sometimes in newspapers, and often in the form of anonymous fliers, these stories warn of children's transfer tattoos impregnated with LSD. The fliers warn that children risk fatal LSD trips from licking these tattoos or absorbing LSD through the skin. The source of the confusion is clear—descriptions of blotter acid (paper printed with cartoon characters) sound similar to descriptions of transfer tattoos. LSD, however, is neither fatal nor absorbed through the skin. The DEA has repeatedly investigated these rumors and found them to be unsubstantiated.[107]

Taking LSD by mouth is the predominant method; injecting LSD is not unheard of, but it is very rare.[110] Injection drug use and LSD use are almost mutually exclusive: injection drug users are usually older (past the age of taking LSD) and are probably looking for a different kind of drug high. Part of the reason adolescents use LSD is that it is easy to conceal and does not require a lot of paraphernalia.

Dealers in LSD have typically given colorful names to their products. There have been green, brown, blue, yellow, and paisley capsules; pink, purple, and yellow wedges; pink, blue, and yellow dots; and pink swirls. Exotic names in earlier years included "Sunshine," "Mighty Quinn," "Blue Cheer," and "LBJ Stay Away."[24, 111] LSD today is often known by the printed emblems or colors of the blotter—"Unicorn," "Blue Blotter," or "Red Roses," for example. Language about taking LSD is equally colorful. In the 1960s and 1970s, LSD users spoke of "dropping hits of acid." Users today still sometimes speak of hits, but also of "dosing," "swinging dose," and "frying."

The DEA speculates there are two basic models of high-level trafficking in LSD. In one, a single close-knit group controls most of the manufacture and distribution in the United States. An inner circle of five to ten individuals controls the manufacturing process, selling 10- to 200-gram lots to a limited outer circle of multigram distributors, who in turn sell smaller quantities to local distributors. In the other model, an individual or a small group of individuals manufacture LSD independently of the northern California source of supply.[107]

Public and private mail services are frequently used at both the upper and lower levels of distribution. Post office boxes under fictitious names may be used, and payment is usually through money-wiring services. Mid-level dealers may travel with a rock group on a national tour to make contacts in local areas.[107] Retail distribution at the lowest level occurs through networks of young adults who are acquainted with each other or have common interests.

In the LSD distribution network described in Chapter 5, the local distributor, a recent high school graduate, ordered LSD from San Francisco through a high school friend. The friend, an LSD user, took a minimal profit. The local distributor sold five to ten sheets a week to each of several high school acquaintances at a 100 percent markup. Some of these acquaintances were themselves LSD users. Others were in college; they wanted to earn spending money and seldom used LSD. These dealers sold sheets or individual doses to acquaintances.

LSD is available throughout the United States. The overall supply appears to have been fairly stable since 1980, although regional fluctuations are common. Several DEA divisions have recently reported increased availability and arrests; others have reported none.[112] Local fluctuations in LSD supply have been associated with the touring schedules of certain rock music bands: when the band plays in a city, a local person touring with the band connects with someone he or she knew in high school. He or she then sells a few sheets of LSD at a minimal profit (for example, getting $45 a sheet after paying $40). There is a brief period of LSD use locally; it subsides quickly when the band leaves town.

The strength of the LSD available in the street market is variable. When production of illegal LSD began, LSD "chemists" such as Stanley Owsley prided themselves on making a product as pure and potent as Sandoz LSD. They also probably gave away free as much LSD as they sold. Other manufacturers were less scrupulous, however, and drug quality overall declined. LSD deteriorates rapidly when exposed to light and oxygen;[12] improper storage quickly reduces potency, and the blotter-acid form of LSD is almost ideally designed to accelerate breakdown. Unprotected, it will probably lose all potency within weeks or months.

The average amount of LSD per dose is reportedly much lower now than was common in the 1960s and 1970s. Testing of confiscated or street-purchased LSD, though, has always been difficult and expensive; it is seldom accorded a high priority. Doses of LSD in the 1960s and 1970s are reported to have been 200 to 250 micrograms. Street samples displayed a wide range in dosage even in 1970, however, from 50 to 300 micrograms.[113, 114] Users were aware that dealers' claims about the strength of their LSD were often inflated, and that the "street mikes" could be six or seven times as high as the real microgram quantity.[115, 116] Even so, users tended to overestimate the amount of LSD they had taken.[117] By the mid-1980s, the average dose is thought to have been 100 to 125 micrograms; in the 1990s it is 20 to 80 micrograms. Some observers believe that lower doses reflect the demands of the marketplace: lower doses mean fewer bad trips.[118]

The purity of LSD is less questionable—drugs sold as LSD have usually been LSD. Nonetheless, it is widely believed that LSD is often adulterated with strychnine or amphetamines. These drugs have stimulant properties that mimic some of LSD's effects, and are cheap or easy to manufacture. Unscrupulous dealers could in theory use these drugs to stretch a small amount of LSD, to enhance poor-quality LSD, or even to sell as LSD. Two factors, however, seem to discourage widespread misrepresentation. First, LSD's effects are so distinctive that a dealer trying to pass off another drug as LSD would soon be out of business. Second, LSD is so potent in such small amounts that stretching it is not necessary. A study of street drugs in 1970, for instance, determined that 14 of 15 samples sold as LSD were indeed LSD.[113] In a 1973 analysis of 405 street samples said to be LSD, 92 percent were LSD; 3 percent contained no drug at all, and 5 percent were adulterated with PCP, DOM (another hallucinogen), or methamphetamine.[24] There is only one reference in the scientific literature to strychnine-contaminated LSD (in Canada).[111] In the hallucinogen black market, it is more common that drugs sold as mescaline and psilocybin mushrooms are really LSD and LSD-treated common mushrooms.[24]

The LSD sold today is almost certainly relatively pure; the blotter and microdot forms of LSD are simply too small to accommodate effective amounts of other drugs. LSD sold in tablets or capsules, as was common in earlier years, could be adulterated, but these forms are seldom found today.

In the 1960s the price of LSD was about $2 per dose of 200 to 250 micrograms. The price per dose has remained stable, although the amount per dose has declined. Nationally the price ranges from $1 to $10 for a dose (retail) and $300 to $4000 for 1000 doses (wholesale).[119] For the consumer, the average price is $3 to $5 for a dose, and sheets of 100 doses are sold for $100 to $250.[120]

3

Adverse Reactions to LSD

Leigh A. Henderson

In the popular mythology, LSD users are prone to violent out-
bursts and bizarre behavior. They may jump off buildings believ-
ing they can fly, stare at the sun until they go blind, tear their eyes
out, or even become homicidal. It is widely believed that an LSD
user may at any moment experience a drug flashback during which
any of these events may recur. The literature on LSD does document some bizarre episodes. Given the millions of doses of LSD
that have been consumed since the 1950s, however, these are rare
indeed.

The medical literature is valuable in documenting the occurrence
of adverse consequences attributed to LSD use. Although it cannot
document every incident in which LSD use was alleged, it is a good
indicator of which adverse effects are common and which are rare.
In the medical literature, a physician observes and reports on a case
or series of cases that have some unusual features, and other physicians then report on similar cases they have seen. Slowly a body of
literature about a disease or a syndrome or a malformation is built.
If the disease or syndrome seems to be linked to a particular risk factor, formal studies may be conducted to confirm the association. Recent drug-related discoveries that evolved in this way are fetal alcohol syndrome and the constellation of symptoms in "crack babies."

There is confusion in the medical literature in distinguishing
normal from abnormal LSD experiences. To some observers, the
extraordinary psychic experience caused by LSD (the LSD trip it-

self) is an "adverse reaction" because it produces an altered mental status. The American Psychiatric Association takes this view, classifying an LSD trip as an "organic mental disorder."[121] Its diagnostic rubric for an LSD trip is *hallucinogen hallucinosis*, the "maladaptive behavioral changes, characteristic perceptual changes, and physical signs due to recent hallucinogen use." To LSD users, however, the altered mental status is the effect that is expected, and it is the reason for using the drug.

Various terms have been used to describe experiences under LSD that the user did not expect, or that were unusual. These include *side effects and complications*,[19, 122–124] *untoward reactions*,[125, 126] *unexpected reactions*,[127] *adverse effects*,[128] *harmful aspects*,[129] and even *LSD misadventures*.[130] The most common term is *adverse reactions*.[25, 131–140] Here the term *adverse reaction* is used to indicate a severe and unpleasant or physically dangerous reaction resulting directly from use of LSD.

The American Psychiatric Association currently identifies three organic mental disorders (apart from hallucinogen hallucinosis) that may result from hallucinogen use: (1) *hallucinogen delusional disorder*, a transient or long-lasting psychotic episode developed during or shortly after hallucinogen use: (2) *hallucinogen mood disorder*, a transient or long-lasting depression or anxiety, or occasionally elation, developed during or shortly after hallucinogen use; and (3) *posthallucinogen perception disorder* (often called "flashbacks"), the reappearance after cessation of hallucinogen use of one or more of the perceptual symptoms, primarily visual, of the intoxication.[121]

The distinction between transient and long-lasting effects is important. Most adverse LSD effects are transient; an analysis in 1967 of the 225 adverse reactions that had been reported in the medical literature revealed that most cases were resolved within forty-eight hours.[141] Transient effects are more easily attributable to LSD than long-lasting effects because they appear within minutes or hours of taking the drug. Psychotic episodes or mood disorders that are long-lasting or that appear long after LSD use are much more difficult to attribute to LSD use alone. Unfortunately, such a diagnosis is not always easy to make.

LSD may be blamed for an adverse reaction even when other factors are involved, simply because its effects are so unusual. For example, one seventeen-year-old man fell into a coma after taking 350 micrograms of LSD, 40 mg of diazepam (Valium), and a "small amount" of methadone.[142] He was diagnosed as having "overdosed" on LSD, although the report noted that 40 mg of diazepam was enough to cause loss of consciousness. The patient had a four-year history of heavy drug use, taking as many as one hundred amphetamine tablets a day, as well as using opium and cocaine and injecting heroin. Drug histories such as these—the combination of LSD with alcohol, marijuana, and other drugs—may account for some of the variety of effects attributed to LSD.

The potential for adverse reactions to LSD was recognized early.[143, 144] Certain (rather benign) hazards were foreseen. These included the dangers of time and space distortion when driving, the "social embarrassment" of mood swings and hallucinations, and "difficulties" associated with impulsive behaviors, wandering, and absentmindedness. Concern about exacerbation of existing psychotic conditions, however, was also expressed.

People with adverse reactions to LSD began to appear at hospital emergency rooms in the middle and late 1960s, when use of illicitly manufactured LSD became widespread. A psychiatric emergency room service in Los Angeles treated one bad trip every two months until September 1965. Then they began to receive referrals from all over the city, averaging ten patients per month for the next six months (12 percent of all patients seen), with three to five phone calls about other patients for each one seen.[117, 145] LSD-related admissions to San Francisco General Hospital soared in the first few months of 1967.[145]

By far the most common adverse reactions to LSD are bad trips and flashbacks. Bad trips are responsible for most hospital or emergency room visits associated with LSD. Flashbacks, although they may occur long after the drug was used, are usually associated with use of LSD rather than other drugs.

Bad Trips

A *bad trip* is an acute anxiety or panic reaction following ingestion of LSD. On a bad trip, painful or frightening feelings are intensified, just as pleasurable sensations are on a good trip. Distortion of the sense of time may cause this experience to seem almost unbearably long. The person may feel that he or she has lost control of the drug and that the trip will never end; he or she may exhibit paranoia or attempt to flee. A bad trip is an acute reaction to LSD, however, and dissipates as the effects of the drug wear off.

As with many elements of LSD use, a bad trip is difficult to define and evaluate. This is because, on an LSD trip, the user is in a highly suggestible emotional state. No LSD trip is wholly "good" or "bad"—any trip can, and probably does, include periods of anxiety or panic as well as periods of pleasure and euphoria. The way these bad moments are handled by the user and by people who are with him or her have a direct effect on the evolution of the trip. Handled in one way, the LSD user may be able to transform the trip into a good experience; handled in another, the bad moments may become overwhelming. Ironically, a trip to the alien and frightening environment of the emergency room may exacerbate a bad trip.

As LSD use became relatively widespread in the late 1960s, the LSD-using subculture developed means of coping with potential bad trips. As the population became more experienced with the drug, persons with anxiety reactions were usually handled by the users' friends rather than taken to emergency rooms.[146] LSD users were cautioned not to trip alone, and most were aware of the importance of "set and setting"—a phrase that occurs repeatedly in the early literature, both medical and lay—in determining the nature of a trip. Some LSD users carried supplies of chlorpromazine (Thorazine, a drug then often used to treat bad trips) or megadoses of vitamin B_3, a home remedy.[147, 148]

In an interesting twist, many LSD users in the 1960s and early 1970s regarded bad trips favorably. Increased self-knowledge was often a goal of LSD use, and the horrors of a bad trip were seen as part of the learning and growing process.[22] In one study, 24 percent of LSD users had experienced bad trips, and 50 percent considered them helpful.[149]

The occurrence of bad trips seems to be most strongly related to personal susceptibility (that is, the state of mind and emotions of the user) and the all-important influence of set and setting. A bad trip probably results from the interaction of the quantity of LSD taken, personal conflicts of the user, and an uncontrolled environment.[116] In several case series, 60 to 70 percent of the patients had preexisting psychiatric illness, personality disorders, or long drug histories.[117, 145, 150–151] Bad trips appear to be unrelated to the number of prior LSD trips.[117, 152] It has been theorized, however, that inexperienced users are probably at greater risk of a bad trip, because they have no basis for comparison of their changed perceptions and are more likely to panic.[116] Strong emotions such as anger also may contribute to the occurrence of a bad trip.[153]

Experience has shown that medication is usually not necessary in the management of a bad trip. Minor tranquilizers or short-acting barbiturates may be used to cut short a panic reaction. Anticholinergic phenothiazines (such as chlorpromazine) should not be used, though, if there is any possibility that the patient has taken not LSD but an anticholinergic drug like PCP, STP, belladonna, or scopolamine.[111] Interaction of these drugs could lead to coma and cardiorespiratory failure.[154] Unfortunately, the external symptoms of LSD and anticholinergic drugs are similar: both are characterized by dilated pupils, reflex hyperactivity, and anxiety symptoms. Anticholinergics also may cause excessive dryness of the mouth and an absence of sweating.[155] Some clinicians have reported their own rough-and-ready diagnostic methods. One relied on the LSD user's dilated pupils and "I feel sorry for you nonusers" smile. Another uses the "palm test," displaying his open palm to the patient from a distance of about eighteen inches and asking for a description of its colors.[156] The LSD user may appear pleased by the question and often describes multiple colors and imagery. The PCP user, in contrast, reacts aggressively and may attack the hand.

In most cases of an LSD-induced bad trip, good results are obtained when the patient is simply reassured that what he or she is experiencing is drug related and will pass as soon as the drug is metabolized.[62, 154, 157–158]

A person experiencing a bad trip will frequently arrive at an emergency room accompanied by a friend or occasionally the police. The hospital setting can increase the sense of fear, and it is important that once the diagnosis is made (usually by history of LSD ingestion), one person be assigned to stay with the patient in a room isolated from the mainstream of emergency room activity so that sensory stimuli can be minimized. It is often possible to "talk down" someone experiencing a bad trip with continual orientation and reassurance that the effects are time limited. In those instances where reassurance is not sufficient, medication with 100–200 mg of intramuscular or oral pentobarbital is usually effective. Antianxiety agents such as diazepam or chlordiazepoxide can also be used in place of pentobarbital. It was formerly common practice to use phenothiazines in treating bad trips, but their use is not usually necessary.[157]

Flashbacks

A spontaneous flashback is the transitory recurrence of perceptions and emotions originally experienced while under the influence of LSD. Flashbacks were documented in an early study of patients undergoing LSD psychotherapy, and they were perceived by those patients as relaxing and helpful.[159] Most flashbacks are episodes of visual distortion that can last for a few seconds to several minutes, or sometimes several hours. Physical symptoms (tingling and numbness) may be present, as may feelings of anxiety, depression, or panic. They are reported to be similar or exact recurrences of the original drug experience,[160] and these episodes are usually recognized as flashbacks by the drug user. A large proportion of those experiencing flashbacks (35 to 57 percent) have reported finding them pleasant (a "free trip"). Very few have sought psychiatric help because of the experience.[160–163]

Flashback incidence rates of 20 to 33 percent have been reported among LSD users in community- and army-based populations.[162, 164–168] Incidence rates as high as 55 to 65 percent have been found in psychiatric and treatment-center populations,[109, 169] although other studies of such populations report rates of 15 to 30 percent.[125, 149, 170–171] Flashbacks usually decrease in frequency and intensity with time. They seldom occur more than a few months after the original trip, but in some persons they have been reported as much as two or three years later.[83, 160, 172] There are isolated case reports of flashback phenomena that are constant rather than episodic. These include the trailing phenomenon[173] and more generalized disturbances, including colored dots and halos.[174]

There is controversy over whether there is a relationship between the extent of LSD use (either total amount of LSD taken or number of LSD trips) and the occurrence of flashbacks. Although flashbacks can occur after a single use of LSD, it is unclear whether those who have used LSD more often are more likely to experience flashbacks. Some studies show no such relationship,[160, 165, 167–169] while others suggest the opposite.[51, 141, 146, 149, 164] One study found that the number and intensity of flashbacks was associated with the number and intensity of bad trips, even when other factors (such as the total number of times LSD was used, and various measures of personality differences) were taken into account.[162]

While flashbacks can occur spontaneously, specific situations can trigger them. For instance, they have been linked repeatedly to the use of marijuana or hashish at some point after an LSD trip.[146, 160, 168–169, 175–177] Flashbacks also may be triggered by movement from a lighted to a dark environment,[169] by emotional stress,[146, 161, 172] or by fatigue.[172] One study found that flashbacks were triggered by pleasant situations in 20 percent of those persons experiencing them, and by unpleasant situations in 21 percent.[160] Finally, many who experience flashbacks can induce them at will (for example, by staring at a blank wall) or can intensify them by concentration.[51, 160–161, 169, 173, 178]

Many theories for the cause of flashbacks have been advanced. Flashbacks are not caused by delayed release of LSD remaining in the brain, as some users have thought, although theories have included various physiologic and biochemical changes.[51, 174, 178] There are numerous psychologic theories.[161, 165] Some users believe that LSD has taught them to use a mode of perception that all humans are capable of, but have not learned. The existence of individual (and possibly genetic) susceptibilities has also been suggested.[169]

Flashbacks may resemble such altered states of consciousness as hypnosis, daydreaming, and sleepwalking.[146] These states can occur naturally and under conditions similar to those that trigger flashbacks—decreased sensory input, stress, fatigue, and relaxation.[179] Persons experiencing flashbacks have been shown to be unusually suggestible to hypnosis.[149] Expectation was demonstrated to be a powerful factor in inducing flashbacks in a study of former LSD users, some of whom had flashbacks while others did not. Both groups were given a drug that they believed would make flashbacks occur (although it would not), and a high proportion of both groups claimed to have flashback symptoms.[179]

Drug therapy for flashbacks has not been particularly successful. Benzodiazepines have been found to reduce the intensity and frequency of flashbacks in some patients.[169] Phenothiazines (for example, chlorpromazine) and haloperidol often intensify or worsen symptoms, at least in the short term, so that patients stop taking them before they can have an effect.[166, 169, 173, 180] Narcotics, barbiturates, and alcohol have been of help for some.[169] Overall, the best treatment is similar to that recommended for acute adverse reactions: the patient should be reassured that the flashbacks are not the result of brain damage and will fade with time, given abstinence from further use of psychedelic drugs, marijuana, and hashish.

LSD and Psychoses

The relationship between LSD and psychoses is a strange one. At one time or another, and often simultaneously, it has been believed that LSD could create a controlled, temporary psychosis suitable for study, that it could cure psychos is, and that it could cause people to become permanently psychotic. Part of the problem lies in the shifting definition of psychosis. In the past few decades, enormous advances have been made in psychiatry in understanding both the nature and causes of mental illness, and LSD was caught up in the evolving understanding, definitions, and diagnoses of mental illness.

It was originally hoped that LSD would cause a controllable, temporary, and reversible form of psychosis, specifically schizophrenia. Understanding the physiologic and biochemical mechanisms of the drug-induced reactions, it was thought, would provide clues to the mechanisms in the naturally occurring illness. Drug therapies counteracting either the mechanisms or the drug-induced mental state might prove to be therapies for the psychosis.[181]

Basically, a psychosis is a mental disorder characterized by distortion of a person's mental capacity, emotions, and ability to recognize reality. Persons who are psychotic typically accept their abnormalities as normal; their behavior represents their routine way of responding to the environment around them. They do not recognize, or are unable to communicate, their difficulties in coping with the ordinary demands of everyday life. A number of different types of psychoses have been described, and their classification and distinguishing features are often in dispute. Psychoses have traditionally been divided into those that are organic and those that are functional. *Organic* psychoses are caused by a physical disorder—a physical abnormality or chemical disturbance. For *functional* psychoses, no such physical cause has been identified. As science learns more about the biochemistry and mechanisms of the brain, psychoses once labeled as functional may be found to have organic causes.

Schizophrenia is the most frequent diagnosis among psychoses. Essentially, it is a disorder in the thinking process characterized by delusions, hallucinations (usually auditory), and extensive withdrawal of the individual's interest from other people and the outside world. Estimates of the extent of schizophrenia in the general population vary widely, in part because definitions are vague. A number of types of schizophrenia have been described, but individuals can exhibit a mix of symptoms, and these can change over time. Further, there is debate about whether syndromes such as manic-depression and paranoia are types of schizophrenia or separate psychoses.

It is easy to see how someone on LSD could be perceived as psychotic or schizophrenic: he or she may behave strangely, talk about things that are not there, or seem irrationally emotional or withdrawn. In fact, until the American Psychiatric Association's third revision of its diagnostic manual in 1980, an LSD reaction would have been classified as schizophrenic.[182] Clearly it is important, when reading the scientific literature, to keep in mind the changing definitions of psychiatric diagnoses.

One of the greatest fears about LSD is that it will cause the user to go insane—to become permanently psychotic, or at least to need lengthy hospitalization. These fears probably began in the early days of LSD, encompassing the 1950s and early 1960s, when use of LSD was largely confined to psychiatric patients (often those who had not responded to other treatments). The other major group taking LSD during this period consisted of volunteers taking part in scientific experiments. These experiments implicitly assumed that participants were "normal," and the reactions they experienced would be those of normal people. One researcher assessed the mental status of fifty-six paid volunteers, however, and found that twenty-three (41%) needed psychiatric treatment; twelve of them had already received some treatment.[183] At a conscious or unconscious level, the researchers felt, most had volunteered for the study for reasons related to their illnesses.

In this crucial period, psychiatrists were concerned with documenting any possible adverse effects of this experimental new drug. Any psychiatric illness developing after LSD treatment was likely to be attributed to LSD, yet the individuals under scrutiny were perhaps the poorest possible group in which to assess LSD's psychiatric aftereffects. By definition, all of the psychiatric patients (and many of the "normal" volunteers) were already ill. On review, reports from this period tend to overemphasize the role of LSD: when patients improved, LSD was given the credit; when they deteriorated, LSD was blamed.

Fears about LSD's potential for inducing or worsening psychiatric problems were expressed quite early. Certain types of psychiatric patients, including patients with schizophrenia, were apt to have severe adverse reactions.[122, 159, 184] Reports of individual cases suggest that LSD can indeed trigger psychotic crises in some individuals and can exacerbate existing psychiatric illness.[5, 122, 125, 141, 171, 184-186]

While there are reports of psychoses requiring weeks or months of hospitalization that are attributed to LSD, however, systematic studies are scarce. In 1960 a survey was conducted of psychiatrists treating patients with LSD or mescaline, and of researchers experimenting with these drugs in volunteer subjects;[122] the survey covered 5,000 patients and more than 25,000 drug ingestions. It was estimated that a psychotic reaction lasting more than forty-eight hours occurred in 0.08 percent of the experimental subjects, and in about twice as many (0.18 percent) psychiatric patients. A similar study conducted in England a decade later covered 4,300 patients and 49,000 drug ingestions.[137] It found a much higher rate (0.9 percent) of psychotic reactions lasting more than forty eight hours. A smaller study found that 3 of 158 patients (2 percent) with schizophrenia had psychotic reactions to LSD that lasted more than twenty-four hours.[138]

Prolonged psychiatric illness appears to be a rare complication of LSD use; if large numbers of such cases exist, they are not documented in the scientific literature. There are several arguments against the theory that LSD directly causes psychiatric illness. For example, LSD is not associated with any specific type of psychosis or group of symptoms—people who exhibit psychosis after LSD use have a wide range of symptoms. Nor has it been possible to show relationships between psychosis and the amount of LSD consumed, the number of LSD trips, or the recency of the last dose.

In discussing the possibility that LSD alone is responsible for an illness, a number of factors must be considered. Was there a preexisting psychiatric illness, or a family history of such illness? Were other drugs used? If so, what is known about their mental and emotional effects? Is it possible the patient took LSD in an attempt to cure himself or herself of psychic distress, or to solve some life problem? Did the psychosis occur immediately after taking LSD—a bad trip that did not resolve with time—or was there a symptom-free interval?

The LSD experience is so exceptional that there is a tendency for observers to attribute any later psychiatric illness to the use of LSD. Thus there are reports of "delayed psychoses" attributed to LSD that have occurred weeks or months, and sometimes even years, after ingestion of the drug.[187, 188] In these reports, there is usually no prior psychiatric diagnosis. The patient or his or her family remember the experience with LSD, and they (as well as the physician) assume that LSD must be the cause of the current illness. The causes or precipitating factors for most cases of mental illness, however, are unknown. While it is human to want to pinpoint a cause or find something to blame, there seems little reason to assume that LSD is more than coincidentally involved in these cases.

Many variables must be considered in diagnosing a psychosis associated with LSD use. These include the extent of drug use, the personal history of the patient, his or her prepsychotic level of functioning, how the psychosis first appeared and what triggered it, and the patient's mental status at examination.[189] Thus it is unrealistic to ascribe to LSD every psychotic episode occurring in a prior user.

Reactions that are prolonged (days to months) and/or require hospitalization are often referred to as "LSD psychoses," and include a heterogeneous population and group of symptoms. Although there are no hard and fast rules, some trends have been noted in retrospective analyses of these patients. There is a tendency for people with poorer premorbid adjustment, a history of psychiatric illness and/or treatment, a greater number of exposures to psychedelic drugs . . . , drug-taking in an unsupervised setting, a history of polydrug abuse, and self-therapeutic and/or peer-pressure-submission motive for drug use, to suffer these complications.

In spite of the impressive degree of prior problems noted in many of these patients, there are occasional reports of severe and prolonged reactions occurring in basically well-adjusted individuals. In the same vein, there are many instances of fairly poorly adapted individuals who suffer no ill effects from repeated psychedelic drug use.[190]

LSD and Schizophrenia

The paradoxical view of LSD as both cause and cure is particularly pronounced with schizophrenia. It became evident very early that attempts to use LSD to induce a "model" schizophrenia would not be fruitful. Comparing an acute, drug-induced state to a chronic behavioral pattern could not produce the hoped-for results.

The psychotomimetic drugs (including mescaline and psilocybin as well as LSD) produce such a wide range of symptoms that it is almost inevitable that some would overlap with the symptoms of schizophrenia. Patients with schizophrenia, though, were easily differentiated from subjects on an LSD trip.[181, 191] Both tended to be withdrawn; however, LSD users, although introspective, liked to have people around and often tripped in groups. A person who is schizophrenic believes his or her hallucinations are real, while the LSD user does not. Auditory hallucinations are the most common form in schizophrenia, but they are rare in LSD users. Both groups have difficulty expressing thoughts. In the LSD user, though, thoughts are related to reality and expressed in the present tense; the user is often concerned about his or her failure to communicate. Persons with schizophrenia are ambiguous and hard to follow in their thinking; they tend to use the past tense. Chronic users of LSD also differed from persons with schizophrenia. Among other indicators, LSD users remained involved with people and maintained their interpersonal skills, while persons with schizophrenia tended to withdraw from others.[192]

In one study patients with schizophrenia were compared to patients whose psychoses were believed to be drug induced.[193] LSD-using patients had fewer delusions; they felt less confused. Their social judgment and reasoning were inferior to those of the patients with schizophrenia, but their memory and attention–spans were better. Both groups had family histories of psychosis and suicide that were similar to each other but different from the general population. The LSD users had high rates of parental alcoholism. These results suggest that a genetic susceptibility to mental illness may predispose an individual to both LSD use and mental illness. A poor family environment resulting from mental illness and/or substance abuse could well exacerbate such a predisposition.

Another study compared four groups of psychiatric patients—drug-using and non-drug-using patients with schizophrenia, and drug-using and non-drug-using patients with other personality disorders.[194] Overall, the groups were most similar when grouped by diagnosis rather than by drug use—that is, patients with schizophrenia were similar to each other regardless of drug use. Patients with schizophrenia who had used drugs were more disturbed than those who had not.

There is some evidence that LSD use might hasten development of schizophrenia in those who are at risk of developing it. Schizophrenia is now believed to be related to several neurotransmitter defects, and because LSD affects neurotransmission, the theory is biologically plausible. Caution is required, however, in making judgments. LSD is used by the same age group in which early-onset schizophrenia appears, and so the two may be associated only coincidentally. In one study, patients with schizophrenia who had used nonopiate drugs (mostly LSD) before the onset of illness experienced onset some four years earlier than patients with schizophrenia who had not used drugs.[195] Their preschizophrenic personalities resembled those of the patients with schizophrenia rather than a group of normal controls; the patients with schizophrenia used a wider variety of drugs and used them more frequently than did the controls. The study provides evidence that earlier onset of schizophrenia may be precipitated by drug use, although it is not possible to single out LSD because of the mixture of drugs used by the subjects.

Self-Destructive and Criminal Behavior

Some of the most lurid stories about LSD fall into this category, although LSD users are by and large passive and tend to avoid mental and physical activity.[72, 117] Whether the stories reported in the media are true or not, they make good headlines; often, however, they are not firsthand objective reports. The medical literature provides a factual basis for some of these stories, and it notes additional, often clarifying, circumstances.

Damage to the eyes from sun-gazing while under the influence of LSD is a popular story. A dozen such cases were reported in the early 1970s; nine were among U.S. army personnel.[196-198] None of the patients was blinded, although they suffered varying degrees of retinal or macular damage. Eye damage can result from the effects of direct or indirect sunlight. The condition is well known and by no means confined to LSD users—it occurs among sunbathers and persons watching solar eclipses without eye protection. LSD could conceivably make sun-gazing more dangerous because it dilates the pupils, admitting more light to the eye. An LSD user may be attracted to the sun because it is bright and because of its religious and spiritual connotations.

Another recurrent story concerns persons tearing out their eyes (self-enucleation) while under the influence of LSD. Incidents of self-enucleation are rare; only twelve have been reported since 1846. In two of these, the patients had used LSD, although they were not under its influence at the time.[199] Both patients, an eighteen-year-old man and a twenty-three-year-old woman, had been raped (the man in a homosexual rape while on his only LSD trip). The woman had a history of extensive multiple drug use and was in a state mental hospital at the time of the enucleation. Both patients removed their right eyes; both cited the biblical verse "And if thy right eye causeth thee to stumble, pluck it out, and cast it from thee."

In perhaps the most bizarre episode attributed to LSD, in the early 1970s a man "under the influence of alcohol and LSD" inserted a twelve-inch rolling pin into his rectum, through his bladder, and into his abdomen.[200] Although the injury was said to be self-inflicted, the man had also been stabbed in the chest. Despite the somewhat mysterious circumstances, the extensive injuries, and the use throughout the report of the phrase "alcohol and LSD," the article was titled "Injury to the Bladder: Unusual Complication of Lysergic Acid Diethylamide." Today, in a society more informed about sexual practices, it seems likely that the man's injuries were inflicted in a sexual encounter. (The patient's recovery from surgery was complete and uneventful.)

LSD has been detected (usually with other drugs) in the blood of persons killed in traffic accidents and in jumping or falling from heights.[201] Some LSD users experiencing a dissociation of the mind and body may interpret this as immortality—the death of the body while the spirit lives on. Their judgment impaired by LSD, they may attempt to fly or walk into the sea.[116]

LSD as a cause of suicide is difficult to evaluate, but probably infrequent. Some alleged LSD suicides may be accidental deaths rather than intentional acts. Most of the early reports of suicide occurred during the period when LSD was used in psychiatric patients. Their interpretation suffers from the same limitations described in the discussion on LSD and psychoses. In a study of 4,300 patients treated with LSD, the rate of suicide was 0.07 percent.[137] This was higher than the 0.01 percent reported in the general population, but similar to the 0.06 percent reported among psychiatrists.

A handful of homicides are alleged to have been committed by persons under the influence of LSD, and "insanity due to LSD" was briefly popular as a criminal defense.[202, 203] Aggression is not a common response to LSD, however, and the involvement of other drugs and, particularly, prior psychiatric illness appear to have been contributing factors. Two reports are briefly summarized here. In the first, a twenty-five-year-old Danish woman became involved with drugs and alcohol (including injected drugs) at the age of nineteen.[204] She came under the influence of "K," a man who forced her to smuggle and maintain an illegal still by threatening to reveal her recent history to her family. She became pregnant by him and had an abortion. She moved several times in an unsuccessful attempt to avoid him. During this period she had five stays in mental institutions; she first felt a wish to kill K before her fourth stay. During the last hospitalization, she received five low-dose (50 microgram) LSD treatments. Despite violent behavior during the treatments, she was released on the third day after the last treatment, feeling confused and disoriented. Immediately after release, she sought out K, carrying a knife in her pocket. They had several drinks, and he apparently tried to have sexual intercourse with her. At this point she stabbed him.

In the second case, a twenty-two-year-old student had used marijuana, amphetamines, and LSD from age twenty.[205] After his first bad trip, he dropped out of school, over his parents' objections. He felt responsible for his father's subsequent heart attack, and for some months he vacillated about what he should do. He took LSD one morning, panicked, and flew home. He briefly saw his parents, who said he appeared normal, but tense and withdrawn. Over the next eight days he continued his flight, traveling to London, Paris, Athens, and Tel Aviv under the belief that he was fleeing a Nazi conspiracy. He was agitated and slept little. In a Tel Aviv café he stabbed and killed a soldier (who he thought was part of the conspiracy) and wounded two other people. He was shot in the chest. The psychosis dissipated while he was in the hospital; he recalled the events, but they did not seem real. During four months in a mental hospital, he was diagnosed as having a paranoid character structure but showed no signs of psychosis.

Health Risks

LSD appears to pose few if any risks to physical health. Because it is usually taken orally, the user does not face the complications of injected drugs—abscesses, phlebitis, endocarditis, hepatitis. (Three cases of hepatitis in persons who did inject LSD, however, have been reported.[110] Their use of other injected drugs was not reported.) The medical literature contains only scattered case reports of serious effects on physical health attributed to LSD. The small number of cases and the lack of a consistent pattern of physical effects lead to the conclusion that these cases are coincidental or, at worst, extremely rare. The literature on cocaine, in comparison, contains numerous references to its role in heart attacks and seizures, as well as damage to the nostrils and nasal septum.

An opportunity arose to study the effects of a massive dose of LSD when a white powder was distributed at a party to guests who assumed it was cocaine.[206] Eight patients were seen within fifteen minutes of inhaling "milligram amounts" of pure LSD (verified in later police analysis of the powder). Five were comatose when first seen and were admitted to the hospital. Two patients walked in themselves and left after spending several hours in the emergency room. Symptoms included vomiting, elevated temperatures, and mild internal bleeding. LSD was detected in the blood or stomach contents of all the patients, in amounts ranging from 2.1 to 26 ng/ml (blood) and 1000 to 7000 micrograms/100 ml (stomach contents). With supportive care, the patients recovered quickly. Those hospitalized were able to converse within four to five hours, and they were normal within twelve hours. No psychologic or physical

ill effects were noted in a year of follow-up examinations of five patients. Most of the five continued to use LSD.

There are less than a handful of reports of cardiovascular events
following shortly after LSD use. Two strokes and a heart attack
were documented in a twenty-year-old woman, a fourteen-year-old
boy, and a seventeen-year-old boy, respectively.[207–209] At least one,
the heart attack victim, had recently taken other drugs—daily marijuana, amphetamines, alcohol, and tobacco, as well as prescription
penicillin.

LSD does not appear to be associated with seizures. At a hospital
in San Francisco, forty nine recreational drug-induced seizures
were seen over a twelve-year period. Cocaine had been used by
thirty-two of the patients, amphetamines by eleven, and heroin or
PCP by eleven. (Eleven patients had used multiple drugs.) LSD had
been used by only one, and that patient had simultaneously used
cocaine and marijuana.[210] In the only other reported instance of
LSD-related seizures, a thirty-two-year-old man experienced
seizures two of the six times he took LSD.[211]

Other syndromes attributed to LSD are equally rare. Rhabdomyolysis (a syndrome including kidney failure that sometimes follows
crush injuries) has been reported in two persons who were re-
strained in straitjackets after taking LSD.[212] This syndrome is reported fairly often in cocaine users, representing up to 5 percent of
cocaine-related emergency room visits.[213] There is a single report of
neuroleptic malignant syndrome after use of alcohol and LSD.[214, 215]
A life-threatening high temperature of 106.4° F (41.3° C) was reported in a man who had ingested a large amount of LSD several
hours previously.[216] The man was known to use amphetamines and
barbiturates as well, and his symptoms were perhaps more consistent with amphetamine overdose.[217]

Chronic or Repeated Use: Effects on the Brain, Personality, and Vision

Long-term chronic abuse of LSD rarely develops. An expert in the
field writes:

> There are several reasons why hallucinogens would not be expected to
> give rise to long-term chronic abuse of the type frequently encountered

with most other mind-altering drugs. First, of course, there is no development of physiological dependence. Second, at least for those hallucinogens for which reliable data are available, daily use leads to rapid build-up of tolerance, such that for practical purposes these drugs cannot be used more than twice a week without losing much of their impact. Equally relevant is the fact that the intense emotional effects of hallucinogens produce a type of psychological satiation which, for most persons, results in much longer intervals between use than is necessary to avoid tolerance effect. A third reason why the hallucinogens appear not suitable for long-term is their lack of dependable effects. Habitual drug users seek to satisfy particular needs—escape, euphoria, anxiety relief, feeling of adequacy, etc. To qualify for long-term use, a drug must consistently produce the type of mood alteration desired. Hallucinogens are quite inconsistent in terms of mood alteration, and in addition, often produce a feeling of increased awareness which is incompatible with the need for escape and withdrawal. The fourth and probably most important reason to expect individuals to decrease rather than increase their hallucinogen use over time is to be found in the characteristics of the drug effect. As described earlier, the major effect of the hallucinogens is to temporarily suspend the normal mode of perception and thinking. The utility of the experience lies in the uniqueness of the new modes of perception and thought which become available under these conditions. However, as one repeats the experience many times, what was initially unique becomes more commonplace and there is a process of diminishing returns. The effect of hallucinogens is indeed "a trip," and trips tend to lose their appeal when repeated too often.[149]

Admission to drug treatment for abuse of LSD is extremely rare. In 1991, only 1.4 percent of drug treatment clients cited use of hallucinogens (other than PCP) as either primary, secondary, or tertiary problems.* In a 1990 random sample of drug treatment facilities nationwide, less than 2 percent of clients had used either LSD or PCP within the thirty days before admission.†

---

*Substance Abuse and Mental Health Services Administration. Client Data System, 1991, unpublished data.

†1990 NIDA Drug Services Research Study, Brandeis University, Institute for Health Policy, unpublished data.

The risk of organic brain damage following continued use of LSD was an area of concern. Evidence of long-term neurologic impairment resulting from the use of abused drugs (other than alcohol and solvents) is scant.[218, 219] Many studies are inconclusive because of the few persons involved. Differences in brain function, personality, and attitudes between LSD users and nonusers appear to be subtle or nonsignificant.[190, 192, 220] No studies, however, have used current psychiatric diagnostic criteria. One controlled study in a psychiatric population found that abstract abilities might have been minimally impaired, but there was no evidence of generalized brain damage.[221] Although it was concluded that minor organic brain damage was possible, later studies by the same investigator did not support this conclusion.[222] Performance on cognitive tasks was normal.

Personality changes in chronic or long-term LSD users are also of interest. In both medical and illicit users, subjects have reported feeling less anxiety.[149, 222] A lack of aggression in long-term LSD users has been noted, but this may be a characteristic of persons who are attracted to LSD rather than a result of its use.[153, 192] One study examined persons who had taken LSD some ten years earlier, either as an adjunct to psychotherapy or in an experimental setting.[149] Nearly one-quarter had continued to use LSD outside the medical setting. The study compared three groups of patients: one had taken LSD only in therapy; one had first used LSD in therapy, then continued to use it nonmedically; the third group had received psychotherapy alone. No patterns of differences in attitudes, beliefs, values, or behaviors were found between patients who had received LSD and those who had not. Large and consistent differences were found, though, between the nonusers and the group who continued to use LSD nonmedically. The LSD users reported a greater appreciation of art and music, were more susceptible to hypnosis, tended to be sensation seeking, and preferred a casual and spontaneous life-style. They viewed themselves as holding attitudes different from most Americans and were likely to feel alienated from society. The existence of such differences in the nonmedical LSD users does not mean that LSD use caused these differences; rather, the two results suggest that LSD attracts a particular type of person.

Vision impairment in long-term users of LSD has been documented in controlled studies as much as two years after ending LSD use.[170, 223] LSD users may have more difficulty in distinguishing colors than nonusers, and LSD users who have experienced flashbacks may have the most difficulty.[170] Some past users have poorer sight in dim light and dysfunctions in peripheral vision as compared to nonusers.[223] Visual acuity and color perception were normal. An earlier study, however, found that chronic LSD users were more sensitive to low-intensity visual stimulation.[192]

Genetic Damage, Birth Defects, and Tumors

The idea that LSD might cause genetic damage first surfaced in 1967.[224] A pattern of chromosome breaks was found in a schizophrenic patient who had been treated with LSD over a four-year period. Similar breaks occurred when LSD was added to a solution containing human cells. There was a flurry of speculation about what this might mean. What would be the effect of broken chromosomes? Did LSD also cause gene mutations, so that children of LSD-using men and women would be deformed? Would it cause cancerous tumors?

Over the next three years, more than one hundred research reports were published in the medical journals. Articles were often accompanied by heated editorials and correspondence. In the first comprehensive review of the evidence, the authors concluded as follows: "We believe that pure LSD ingested in moderate doses does not damage chromosomes in vivo, does not cause detectable genetic damage, and is not a teratogen [causing birth defects] or a carcinogen in man."[225] A similar review appeared a year later, incorporating another forty studies that had appeared in the interim.[226] Its conclusions were similar.

Although LSD can induce chromosome breaks both in laboratory cell cultures and in the circulating blood cells of LSD users, it has no lasting effect on genes or chromosomes. This is explained by the finding that no such changes occur in the bone marrow, where new blood cells are produced.[227] When the affected cells die, they are replaced by normal cells over several months. Many substances cause breaks in chromosomes without lasting harm to the user. LSD does not cause the type of genetic damage that can be inherited by a user's children.

The effect of LSD on human pregnancy and its outcomes is difficult to study. In addition to multiple drug use, drug-using mothers are apt to have poor prenatal care and poor nutrition. LSD use during pregnancy does not appear to harm the developing fetus.[228–231] In a study of the effect of LSD on human pregnancy, the rates of spontaneous abortions, premature births, and birth defects were normal; however, doses were low and infrequent (administered therapeutically).[232] A subgroup that used LSD and other drugs nonmedically showed a higher rate of spontaneous abortion, but the number of subjects was too small for statistical analysis. In another study, teenage mothers who used LSD and other nonopiate drugs had an increased incidence of early labor and preterm delivery, although there was no teratogenic effect.[229] A study of infants whose parents used LSD (among other drugs) found no increased chromosomal breakage or rearrangement.[114] Although occasional case reports of birth defects attributed to LSD (either alone or in combination with other drugs) continue to appear,[233–235] systematic studies of humans and animals have failed to show a teratogenic risk for LSD.[225–226, 236–238]

4

LSD Use and LSD Users

Questions and Answers About LSD

Leigh A. Henderson

In this chapter, the most recent national data are used to answer the key questions about LSD and its use today. Who uses it? Is use increasing? How many people suffer adverse effects? How easy is it to get LSD? What do adolescents think about the drug?

Drug use and the problems it causes are monitored using two basic approaches. Drug use in the general population is measured by taking surveys—asking a scientifically chosen group of people questions about the drugs they use or have used. Government agencies conduct or support several national drug surveys of people living in households, of secondary school and college students, of people who have been arrested, and of people entering drug treatment. Other surveys are conducted by states (for example, of middle school students) or by scientific researchers (for example, of pregnant women).

When the goal of a survey is to find out what drugs people use and how often they use them, questions like the following are asked about a number of drugs:

Have you ever used [drug]?
Did you use [drug] in the past year?
Did you use [drug] in the past month?
How old were you when you first used [drug]?
When was the most recent time you used [drug]?

On average, how often in the past year did you use [drug]?
In the past month, on how many days did you use [drug]?

Other questions ask about the method used to take the drug (for example, sniffing, injecting, or smoking), perceptions of the danger and availability of various drugs, and so on.

The statistics most commonly reported from surveys are *prevalence rates*, the proportion of people who have used a drug. *Lifetime* prevalence includes all people who have ever tried a drug, even once. *Annual* prevalence includes only those people who used the drug within the past year. *Past-month* prevalence includes only those people who used the drug within the previous month. The different prevalence rates are used for different purposes: lifetime prevalence shows how far drug use has penetrated a population or community, and annual and past-month prevalence rates are used to indicate the extent of more recent drug use. It might be thought that past-month rates would best indicate current use; however, the numbers of people reporting use in the past month can be very small. The meaning of small numbers is statistically difficult to interpret, so annual rates are often used instead.

The second way of looking at drug use is to look at the harm that it does. To do this, points of contact between the drug user and social institutions are monitored. These institutions include emergency rooms, medical examiners' and coroners' offices, treatment programs, and the judicial system. They provide information on the drugs (and combinations of drugs) that cause illness or death, that cause people to seek help for their drug use, and that are associated with crime and violence.

Because drug use involves illegal behaviors data about it must be carefully assessed. Does the population surveyed effectively represent all users of a drug, or does it reflect drug use within a limited population? Some groups that may have high rates of drug use (for example, the homeless) are difficult to identify and interview using conventional survey techniques. Groups that are more easily accessible (for example, people living in conventional households and willing to be interviewed) may have relatively low rates of drug use.

The truthfulness of answers to questions about illegal behaviors is always uncertain. In general, underreporting of drug use is believed to occur, although some believe that adolescents may *overreport* drug use. Much can depend on the survey method. Is the questionnaire administered in private, or are other people (classmates, teachers, family members) in the room? Does the interviewer ask the questions, or is the questionnaire self-administered? These and other problems may account for some of the variation observed from survey to survey among apparently similar groups. While the absolute prevalence rates may vary, however, changes in reported drug use will still reflect the underlying situation if the amount of underreporting remains fairly constant over time.

Major Data Sources

The major data sources used here include (1) the National Household Survey on Drug Abuse, a survey of the use of illicit drugs, alcohol, and tobacco in the household population aged twelve and older; (2) *Monitoring the Future: A Continuing Study of the Lifestyles and Values of Youth* (often called the "High School Senior Survey," although the study also includes young adults, college students, and eighth- and tenth-grade students); (3) the Drug Abuse Warning Network (DAWN), a sentinel system monitoring acute drug-related problems through emergency rooms and medical examiners' and coroners' offices; (4) the Drug Use Forecasting Project (DUF), a sentinel system monitoring patterns of drug use in arrestees; and (5) the Community Epidemiology Work Group (CEWG). The Appendix to this volume contains details about study populations and design.

Questions and Answers About LSD

How Many People Use LSD?

LSD and other hallucinogens are far less widely used than are other available drugs (Table 1). An estimated 12.0 million people in the household population aged twelve and over (5.8 percent) reported having tried LSD at least once. This is significantly fewer than the 67.3 million who have tried marijuana, the 25.4 million who reported nonmedical use of prescription drugs, and the 23.3 million who have tried cocaine. Of the six major illicit drug classes shown in Table 1, hallucinogens rank fourth in prevalence in every age group. Among adults (all persons over eighteen), only heroin and inhalants have been tried by fewer people than hallucinogens.

TABLE 1

Lifetime Prevalence of the Use of Various Drugs in U.S.
Households, Persons Aged 12 and Older,
by Age Group, 1991

Drug	12–17 (%)	18–25 (%)	26–34 (%)	35+ (%)	Total (%)
U.S. population (in thousands)	20,145	28,496	38,737	115,481	202,859
Alcohol	46.4	90.2	92.4	87.4	**84.6**
Any illicit drug[a]	20.1	54.7	61.8	27.3	**37.0**
Marijuana/hashish	13.0	50.5	59.5	23.7	**33.2**
Psychotherapeutics[b]	7.5	17.9	20.0	9.6	**12.5**
Cocaine	2.4	17.9	25.8	6.8	**11.5**
Inhalants	7.0	10.9	9.2	2.5	**5.4**
Hallucinogens	3.3	13.1	15.5	5.2	**8.1**
LSD	2.6	9.7	10.8	3.8	**5.8**
PCP	1.1	4.2	8.0	2.4	**3.6**
Psilocybin	0.5	4.0	5.9	2.1	**2.9**
Mescaline	0.1	2.6	5.3	2.6	**2.8**
Peyote	0.2	0.8	2.3	1.7	**1.5**
Ecstasy (MDMA)	0.5	2.8	1.5	0.4	**1.0**
Heroin	0.3	0.8	1.8	1.5	**1.3**

Source: National Household Survey on Drug Abuse, 1991.
[a]Nonmedical use at least once of marijuana, hashish, cocaine (including crack), inhalants, hallucinogens (including PCP), heroin, or psychotherapeutics.
[b] Nonmedical use of any prescription-type stimulant, sedative, tranquilizer, or analgesic; does not include over-the-counter drugs.

Among adolescents, hallucinogen use is surpassed by inhalant use, and it ranks ahead of only cocaine and heroin.

Figure 1 shows annual and past-month prevalence rates for persons aged fourteen to thirty-two. The data show that about six percent of the interviewees aged eighteen to twenty-two had used LSD in the year before the survey. Persons just out of high school (19 to 20-year-olds) were most likely to be current LSD users—that is, to have used

FIGURE 1

Annual and Past-Month Prevalence of LSD Use by Age, Adolescents (Grades 8, 10, and 12) and Young Adults (Aged 19–32), 1992.

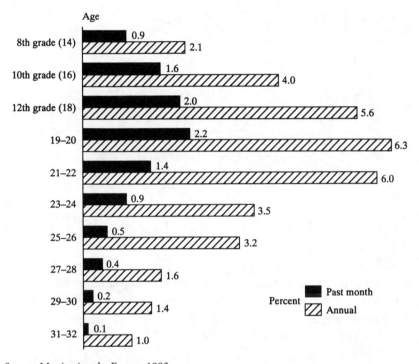

Source: Monitoring the Future, 1992.

LSD in the month before the survey (2.2 percent). They were followed by high school seniors at 2.0 %, and tenth graders at 1.6 percent. Use of LSD decreases at higher ages; after age 22, less than one percent of those interviewed had used LSD within the prior month.

What Demographic Group (Sex, Race, and Socioeconomic Status) Is Most Likely to Use LSD?

LSD appeals mainly to a limited demographic population. The typical LSD user is a white male in his late teens or early twenties, probably from a more affluent background than users of other drugs. Male users outnumber female by two or three to one. The proportion of male LSD users ranges from 63 percent in the Household Survey to 72 percent in DAWN and 76 percent among

TABLE 2

Prevalence of LSD Use, by Parents' Education,
High School Seniors, 1992

Parental Education[a]	Lifetime (%)	Annual (%)
1.0–2.0 (low)	7.6	3.3
2.5–3.0	8.3	5.2
3.5–4.0	8.6	5.7
4.5–5.0	8.7	5.8
5.5–6.0 (high)	9.4	7.0

Source: Monitoring the Future, 1992.

[a] Average of both parents' education: 1 = completed grade school or less; 2 = some high school; 3 = completed high school; 4 = some college; 5 = completed college; 6 = post-college graduate or professional school. Missing data allowed for one parent.

the arrestees in DUF. Smaller state-level surveys and other studies show a similar pattern.

LSD users are predominantly white. The proportion of the LSD-using population that is white varies widely in the national surveys, however, from 63 percent in DUF to 78 percent in DAWN and 93 percent in the Household Survey. This range of estimates reflects the different populations studied. The Household Survey data, which are the most representative of the overall U.S. population, indicate that in 1991 57 percent of LSD users were white males and 35 percent were white females; the remaining eight percent included all other racial and ethnic groups. The arrestee population in DUF has a higher proportion of black and Hispanic LSD users, probably because these groups are overrepresented in the metropolitan prison population. DAWN is also based in metropolitan areas, where black and Hispanic populations are likely to be concentrated; it also probably overrepresents black and Hispanic populations. *Monitoring the Future* calculated that the annual prevalence of LSD use for the period 1985–1989 was 7.0 percent, 3.9 percent, 1.3 percent, and 0.3 percent for white males, white females, black males, and black females, respectively.[8]

Low socioeconomic status, often associated with high rates of drug use, is usually measured by income, education, or type of job. Many LSD users are in high school or college, however, and thus have not yet established these measures. *Monitoring the Future* used

TABLE 3

Annual Prevalence of the Use of Various Drugs, by College Plans, High School Seniors, 1992

Drug	Complete 4 yrs college (%)	No college or under 4 yrs (%)
Alcohol	75.9	79.7
Marijuana	19.4	27.5
Stimulants[a]	6.1	9.7
LSD	4.8	7.6
Cocaine	2.4	5.1
Crack	1.0	2.6

Source: Monitoring the Future, 1992.

[a] Annual prevalence not available. 30-day prevalence presented here.

the level of education of parents to indicate a student's socioeconomic status; the study found that LSD use was markedly higher among students whose parents were more highly educated (Table 2). In contrast, use of cocaine, crack cocaine, and prescription drugs was greatest among students whose parents were less well-educated. Marijuana use appeared to be less dependent on parental education.

Students' plans for college were used as another indicator of socioeconomic status. Students not planning to attend four years of college had higher rates of use of all drugs (Table 3). While the use of alcohol was not very different in the two groups of students, the gap was wider for illicit drugs. Thus marijuana use among students with four-year college plans was 30 percent lower than in those without; LSD use was 37 percent lower. For drugs such as crack cocaine or PCP, however, prevalence of drug use was 50 to 60 percent lower in those with college plans. These data could be interpreted as indicating that LSD users place a higher value on education than users of harder drugs.

How Old Are People When They Start Using LSD?

First use of LSD is most likely to occur in adolescence. Figure 2 shows the cumulative distribution of first use of hallucinogens (the Household Survey) and LSD (DUF). Of the LSD users interviewed in the Household Survey, one-quarter had already tried hallucinogens by age fifteen, one-half by age seventeen, and 75 percent by age nineteen. The pattern of use in the arrestee population in DUF is similar, although the first use of LSD among arrestees is about a year earlier than in the household population. Data from *Monitoring the Future* support this; Figure 3 shows the proportion of youngsters in a given school grade who try a drug for the first time. Thus adolescents are most likely to try LSD between the 10th and 12th grades, when most are between the ages of fifteen and eighteen.

Is LSD More Common in Some Parts of the Country Than Others?

LSD is used throughout the United States, although local fluctuations in use are common. While all DAWN metropolitan areas reported some LSD-related emergency room visits in 1990, cities in

FIGURE 2
Age at First Use of LSD, Household Population Aged 12 and Older, 1991, and Metropolitan Arrestees, 1989

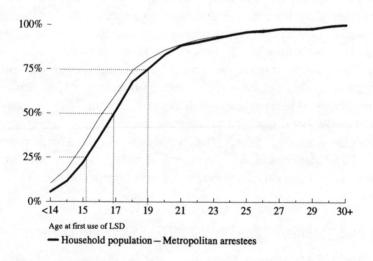

Source: National Household Survey on Drug Abuse, 1991; Drug Use Forecasting Project, 1989.

FIGURE 3

School Grade at First Use of Various Drugs, High School Seniors, 1992

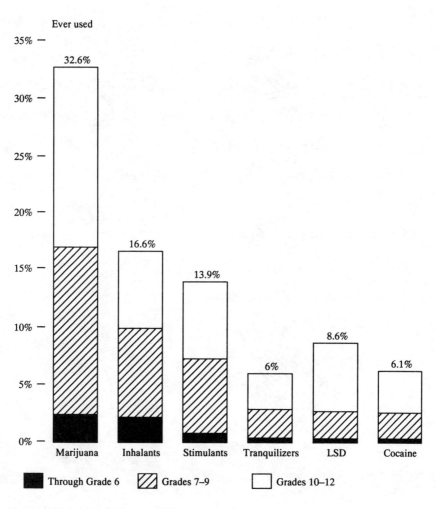

Source: Monitoring the Future, 1992.

western states reported more LSD-related emergency room episodes than other cities. Reports from the CEWG (based on treatment program data and the observations of school and police officials) and DUF data also suggest that LSD use is more common in the West. In 1989, the five cities reporting LSD use by more than

FIGURE 4
Number of Times Various Drugs Were Used, High School Seniors, 1992

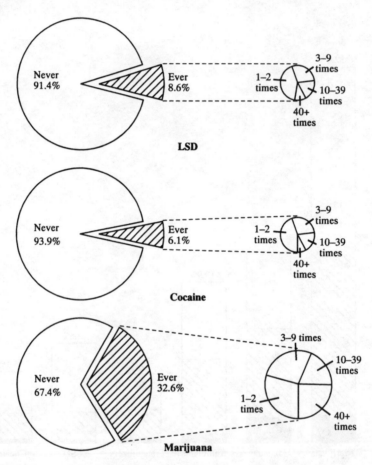

Source: Monitoring the Future, 1992.

25 percent of arrestees were all in the Pacific and Mountain census regions (Portland, San Diego, Los Angeles, Phoenix, and San Jose). In contrast, none of the ten cities reporting LSD use by less than 10 percent of arrestees were in the West.

What Is the Course of an Individual's LSD "Career"?

The typical LSD user will try the drug only a few times, and will stop using it completely within a short period. LSD use is often made up of only one or two experiences. More than 90 percent of high school seniors have never tried LSD (Figure 4). Of those who have tried it (8.6 percent), nearly half have used it only once or twice, and only one-quarter have used it more than ten times. This pattern is strikingly similar to cocaine use among high school seniors, but very different from marijuana use. Thirty-three percent of high school seniors have tried marijuana; one-third of these have used it only once or twice, and nearly half have used it more than ten times. In other words, 1 in 50 students has used LSD on ten or more occasions, compared to seven of 50 who have smoked marijuana more than ten times. Less than 1 in 100 will use LSD more than forty times, compared to seven in 100 who will use marijuana that often.

Rates of use for all drugs decline as individuals develop family and work roles.[239] *Monitoring the Future* tracks the continuing drug use of high school seniors as they grow older. The survey found that the LSD career is short, with use declining in each successive age group after age 20 (Table 4). In contrast, use of cocaine and even marijuana continued to grow after high school. The annual and past-month prevalence rates of LSD use peaked at ages 19 to

TABLE 4

Annual and Past-Month Prevalence of the Use of Various Drugs by Age Group, Adults Aged 18-32, 1992

	Within past month			Within past year		
Age	LSD (%)	Cocaine (%)	Marijuana (%)	LSD (%)	Cocaine (%)	Marijuana (%)
18	2.0	1.3	11.9	5.6	3.1	21.9
19–20	2.2	1.0	14.1	6.3	3.7	26.9
21–22	1.4	1.6	14.7	6.0	5.1	26.9
23–24	0.9	1.9	12.5	3.5	6.5	26.6
25–26	0.5	2.3	12.6	3.2	6.6	23.5
27–28	0.4	2.5	12.0	1.6	7.2	21.2
29–30	0.2	2.2	12.2	1.4	6.7	20.1
31–32	0.1	2.1	11.3	1.0	5.7	17.7

Source: Monitoring the Future, 1992.

20, then declined rapidly. Marijuana use did not peak until the early twenties, and cocaine use continued to increase into the late twenties. The prevalence of marijuana use had declined only slightly by age thirty-one or thirty-two, and use of cocaine continued at a constant rate. LSD use had stopped almost completely by that age.

How Many LSD Users Are Taken to a Hospital Emergency Room?

Severe adverse reactions to LSD are rare, and death due to an overdose of LSD is essentially unknown. DAWN contains three reports of deaths in 1991 linked to LSD, less than one-tenth of one percent of all reported drug-associated deaths. In at least two of these deaths, LSD was used in combination with other drugs. DAWN estimates that LSD use was involved in a total of 3,421 trips to emergency rooms in 1989, 3,869 in 1990, and 3,912 in 1991 (Figure 5). There is a well-defined seasonal pattern: LSD-related emergency room episodes are most frequent in the third quarter of the year (July through September), during school vocation.

The small increase in the absolute number of LSD-related episodes probably reflects a growing population. The rate of occurrence of such episodes, which takes into account the larger population, has remained fairly constant; LSD is consistently cited in only four or five of every 100,000 drug-related emergency room visits. Some episodes involve more than one drug, so that LSD represents less than one percent of all the drugs named in emergency room visits.

Why Are LSD Users Sometimes Taken to Emergency Rooms, and What Are the Results of Such a Visit?

Most emergency room episodes appear to have been bad trips that resolved quickly. The most frequent reason for the emergency room visit was an overdose or unexpected reaction; this was cited in 72.5 percent of the 1991 episodes involving LSD. In 70.1 percent of these episodes, the patient was treated and released; this was a higher rate of release than for any other drug.

Most LSD-related emergency room episodes involve additional drugs—usually marijuana/hashish, alcohol, or both. The propor-

FIGURE 5

Trends in Number and Rate of LSD-Related Emergency Room Visits, by Quarter, 1989–1992

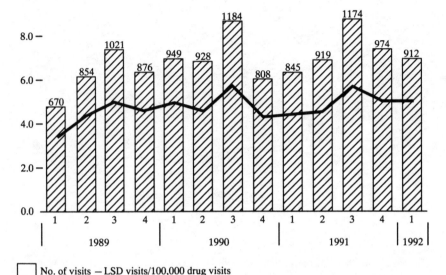

No. of visits — LSD visits/100,000 drug visits

Source: Drug Abuse Warning Network, 1989–1992.

tion involving other drugs increased steadily from 36 percent in 1976 to 57 percent in 1991. In 1991, 30 percent of the episodes involved one other drug as well as LSD, and 27 percent involved two or more additional drugs.

Is LSD Use Increasing?

The data available in *Monitoring the Future* do not support a major increase in LSD use (Figure 6). In every year since 1975 (when the survey began), about two percent of high school seniors had used LSD in the prior month. Lifetime use of LSD fell from the recorded high of 11.3 percent in 1975 to 7.2 percent in 1986, then increased slightly, reaching 8.8 percent in 1991. Both annual and lifetime prevalence are well below the peaks recorded in the late 1970s and early 1980s. The slight increase in the prevalence of past-month LSD use occurred in a period (1985–1992) in which drug and alco-

FIGURE 6

Trends in Prevalence of LSD Use, High School Seniors, 1975–1992

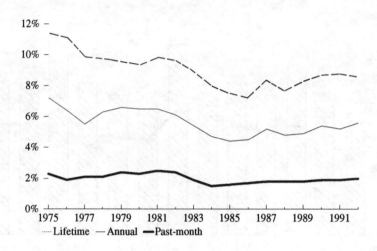

Source: Monitoring the Future, 1975–1992.

hol use among high school students generally fell (Table 5). The slightly increased use of LSD is an exception to the general trend.

Is the Age at Which LSD Is First Used Getting Lower?

Unfortunately, it is difficult to answer this question conclusively. Data have not been routinely collected on children younger than high school seniors. Even current data on drug use among middle or elementary school children are inadequate. Both the Household Survey and DAWN can be used to infer something about trends in the age of LSD users, but the results could be interpreted as conflicting.

For Figure 7, the year in which hallucinogens were first used was calculated for each LSD user in the Household Survey; then the average age of all those who began using hallucinogens in that year was computed. Thus in 1970, for example, interviewees with ages ranging from twelve to thirty-two first used hallucinogens; their av-

TABLE 5

Trends in Current Use (Use in the Past Month) of Various Drugs, High School Seniors, 1975-1992.

Drug	1975 (%)	1980 (%)	1985 (%)	1990 (%)	1992 (%)
Any illicit drug[a,b]	30.7	37.2	29.7	17.2	14.4
Marijuana/hashish	27.1	33.7	25.7	14.0	11.9
Stimulants[b,c]	8.5	12.1	6.8	3.7	2.8
Inhalants[d]	NA	2.7	3.0	2.9	2.5
Hallucinogens[e]	4.7	4.4	3.8	2.3	2.3
LSD	2.3	2.3	1.6	1.9	2.0
PCP	NA	1.4	1.6	0.4	0.6
Sedatives[c]	5.4	4.8	2.4	1.4	1.2
Tranquilizers[c]	4.1	3.1	2.1	1.2	1.0
Cocaine	1.9	5.2	6.7	1.9	1.3
Heroin	0.4	0.2	0.3	0.2	0.3
Alcohol	68.2	72.0	65.9	57.1	51.3

Source: Monitoring the Future, 1992.

Note. NA = data not available.

[a]Use at least once of marijuana, hallucinogens, cocaine, and heroin, or any use of other opiates, stimulants, barbiturates, methaqualone (excluded since 1990), or tranquilizers not under a doctor's orders.

[b]Beginning in 1982, the question about stimulant use was revised to exclude inappropriate reporting of nonprescription stimulants. The prevalence rate dropped as a result of this methodological change.

[c]Drug use not under a doctor's orders.

[d]Data adjusted for underreporting of amyl and butyl nitrites.

[e]Data adjusted beginning in 1979 for underreporting of PCP.

erage age was 18.3. In 1991, the range was from twelve to twenty-five, and the average was 17.6. Clearly, the average age at which LSD is first used has changed very little, hovering consistently at seventeen to eighteen years old. Also consistent is the lower limit of the age range; while it is disturbing that there are current reports of children as young as nine using LSD, it is not a new development.

From DAWN data, it can be calculated that the proportion of younger children in LSD-related emergency room episodes changed dramatically beginning in 1984 (Figure 8). Historically,

FIGURE 7

Age Range and Average Age of First Use of Hallucinogens, LSD-Using Household Population Aged 12 and Older, 1965–1991

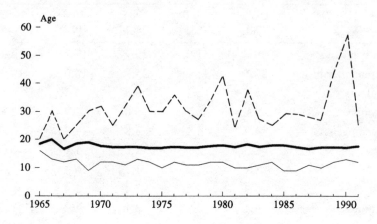

Source: National Household Survey on Drug Abuse, 1990–1991.

80 to 90 percent of all patients in LSD-related emergency room episodes have been below age thirty. In 1984, patients under eighteen made up 25 percent of the total; by 1990 this proportion had increased to 38 percent. This increase was balanced primarily by a decrease in the proportion of patients in their thirties. Unfortunately, the nature of DAWN data makes it impossible to identify the driving force behind the change. The data could signify that fewer people in their thirties were using LSD (as data from other sources seems to support), driving up the proportion of youths. Conversely, they could equally represent an increase in LSD use among youths, forcing down the proportion of those over thirty.*

---

*DAWN data are not strictly comparable over time. The data in Figure 8 represent, for 1976–1985, a group of hospitals that reported consistently throughout the period; for 1986–1989, all reporting hospitals; and for 1990, estimates for the continental U.S. In 1991 the reported age breakdown was changed, and the data are not comparable with earlier years.

FIGURE 8
Trends in the Age Distribution of LSD-Related Emergency Room Visits, 1976–1990

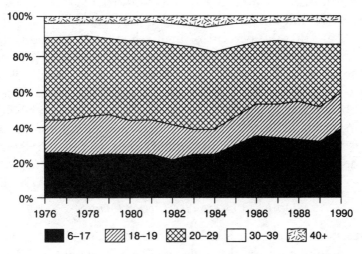

Source: Drug Abuse Warning Network, 1976–1990.

How Easy Is It To Get LSD?

The ease of getting LSD is difficult to measure with any precision. In the 1991 Household Survey, 27 percent of all respondents (all ages) reported that LSD would be fairly or very easy to obtain. The proportion was higher, 44 percent, among those who had actually tried LSD. In 1975, when the *Monitoring the Future* survey was begun, forty-six percent of high school seniors reported that LSD would be fairly or very easy to get. That proportion had dropped to 32 percent by 1978. It remained at 30 to 35 percent for the next decade, falling as low as 29 percent in 1986. In recent years, LSD appears to have become somewhat more easily available; by 1992, about 45 percent of seniors again reported that LSD would be fairly easy to get. In comparison, marijuana has been seen as readily available by 80 to 90 percent of high school seniors throughout the period 1975 to 1992. Cocaine has consistently been seen as more readily available than LSD since 1978; between 1986 and 1992, 50 to 60 percent of seniors have said cocaine would be fairly or very easy to get.

What Do Adolescents Think of LSD? Have Attitudes Changed Over Time?

The attitudes of high school seniors toward LSD are generally conservative and have varied only a few percentage points since 1975. More than 90 percent of high school students have never tried LSD. About 80 to 85 percent believe that taking LSD regularly could cause "substantial physical or mental harm." Nearly 90 percent believe that LSD should not be taken, even once or twice, by persons over eighteen. About 60 to 70 percent believe that LSD should be illegal even for private consumption. The changes in reported availability of LSD appear to be unrelated to attitude.

Do LSD Users Use Other Drugs?

LSD users are likely to use a number of legal and illegal drugs as well. Among the several drugs classified as hallucinogens, LSD has been tried by the largest proportion of people (see Table 1, page 000). People who have used one hallucinogen, however, are likely to have used others as well. On average, hallucinogen users have tried two different types.

The extensive use of drugs other than hallucinogens by LSD users is demonstrated in Table 6. Nearly all persons who have tried LSD have also tried alcohol, cigarettes, and marijuana. Eighty percent have tried cocaine, half have used prescription stimulants nonmedically, and 30 to 40 percent each have tried inhalants or used prescription sedatives, tranquilizers, or analgesics nonmedically. Heroin use among LSD users is less common, but still exceeds that in the general population.

Even among adolescents aged twelve to seventeen, multiple drug use by LSD users is common. Most have used alcohol, marijuana, and cigarettes; half have tried cocaine, and half have tried inhalants. Use of prescription drugs (stimulants, tranquilizers, analgesics, or sedatives) is less common, perhaps because of their limited availability, but still occurs in 20 to 40 percent of adolescent LSD users. Use of heroin is relatively rare in this group, but is high compared to the general population.

TABLE 6

Lifetime Prevalence of Use of Other Drugs by LSD Users,
Household Population Aged 12 and Older,
by Age Group, 1991

Drug	12–17 (%)	18–25 (%)	26–34 (%)	35+ (%)	Total (%)
N	176	559	688	284	1,707
(weighted, in thousands)	(516)	(2,759)	(4,200)	(4,391)	**(11,866)**
Alcohol	97.6	99.9	100.0	99.9	**99.8**
Marijuana/ hashish	92.9	98.4	99.9	99.2	**99.0**
Cigarettes	94.9	97.3	95.9	96.9	**96.6**
Cocaine	53.6	75.4	88.5	79.2	**80.5**
Stimulants	45.1	41.8	57.9	55.2	**52.6**
Tranquilizers	28.7	33.7	49.2	39.0	**40.9**
Analgesics	28.8	38.1	39.7	40.5	**39.2**
Inhalants	48.1	43.2	42.3	29.4	**38.0**
Sedatives	19.9	22.6	41.4	39.3	**35.3**
Heroin	5.5	4.5	11.7	24.0	**14.3**

Is There a Progression in Drug Use, and Where Does LSD Fit?

LSD is probably neither the first nor the only drug an adolescent uses. The "gateway" model of drug use has been well defined[239, 240] (although not universally accepted); it proposes a progression in drug use from the milder legal drugs (beer, wine, cigarettes) to stronger legal drugs (hard liquor, inhalants, over-the-counter stimulants and tranquilizers) and mild illegal drugs (marijuana and hashish). Use of hallucinogens and abuse of prescription drugs may follow. The model does not imply that use of the milder drugs inevitably leads to harder drug use, but it does state that users of the harder drugs have used—and probably still do use—the milder substances. Thus LSD users are likely to use a number of legal and illegal drugs as well.

The drugs most commonly used by adolescents, in order of initiation, are alcohol, marijuana/hashish, inhalants, amphetamines (stimulants), barbiturates, and hallucinogens. In *Monitoring the Future*, marijuana, inhalants, amphetamines, and barbiturates were more likely to be used first in eighth grade than in the tenth or twelfth grade. LSD and cocaine were most commonly introduced later, in tenth or twelfth grade (see Figure 3, page 000). DUF data show a similar pattern (Figure 9): introduction to alcohol, marijuana, and inhalants occurred at ages twelve to fourteen; to barbiturates, amphetamines, and LSD at age sixteen; and to cocaine not until age eighteen.

Different drugs are popular among different age groups (Table 7). Alcohol is the most prevalent at any age. In *Monitoring the Future*, inhalants were the most popular drug in the eighth grade, probably because their quasi-legal status makes them easy to get. By tenth grade, marijuana was the most prevalent drug, followed by the nonmedical use of prescription stimulants and inhalants. Inhalant use continues to decline through high school, but the use of illicit drugs and the nonmedical use of prescription stimulants and tranquilizers continues to rise throughout the same period.

FIGURE 9
Median Age at First Use of Various Drugs, Arrestees, 1989

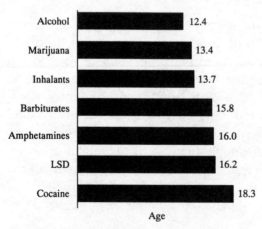

	Age
Alcohol	12.4
Marijuana	13.4
Inhalants	13.7
Barbiturates	15.8
Amphetamines	16.0
LSD	16.2
Cocaine	18.3

Source: Drug Use Forecasting Project, 1989.

TABLE 7
Annual Prevalence of the Use of Various Drugs,
by School Grade, 1992

Drug	8th grade (%)	10th grade (%)	12th grade (%)
Alcohol	53.7	70.2	76.8
Marijuana/hashish	7.2	15.2	21.9
Stimulants[a]	6.5	8.2	7.1
Inhalants	9.5	7.5	6.2
LSD	2.1	4.0	5.6
Tranquilizers[a]	2.0	3.5	2.8
Cocaine	1.5	1.9	3.1
Heroin	0.7	0.6	0.6

Source: Monitoring the Future, 1992.
[a]Drug use not under a doctor's orders.

Summary

The primary concerns about LSD are that its use is increasing, and that LSD users today are younger than in the past. Neither of these concerns gains much support from the data available. Rather, after the intense interest and experimentation it generated in the late 1960s and early 1970s, LSD use has settled into an entrenched pattern among a limited population. In some ways, LSD use resembles an endemic disease—a disease that continuously circulates at low levels in a population.

The level of LSD use has varied little between the late 1970s and early 1990s. Although local outbreaks of LSD use are periodically reported in the media, evidence of a current nationwide epidemic is not compelling. Some communities across the United States have recently reported increased LSD use, but others report none. Regional fluctuations in supply and demand for this drug seem to be part of its entrenched pattern, and significant increases in LSD supplies have not been reported at the national level in recent years.

National surveys suggest that LSD users are usually white, male, and middle to upper class. The user's interest in first trying LSD peaks in late adolescence. He or she has probably used alcohol and marijuana, and possibly inhalants and over-the-counter drugs. He or she will probably use LSD only a few times.

The average user tries LSD at age seventeen; by definition, then, half the people who try LSD do so *before* they are seventeen. LSD use at ages as low as nine has been consistently reported over the past fifteen to twenty years. Incidence at this age is extremely low, however, and available data do not show it to be increasing. Most high school students who report using LSD try it only once or twice. Even among the small number who continue use beyond one or two experiments, most will have stopped stop by the time they reach their early twenties. Only a small percentage continue LSD use into their thirties.

LSD use only rarely results in a reaction requiring emergency medical care. In the majority of cases where this occurs, the individuals are treated and released; prolonged hospitalization is not required. Furthermore, most of these cases involve other drugs as well as LSD.

LSD is only one of many drugs to which adolescents are exposed in today's society. It is very likely that an adolescent using LSD *will have already tried* (and perhaps be continuing to use) other drugs as well. LSD use among high school students is less frequent than alcohol, marijuana, or even cocaine use. It is also used less frequently than over-the-counter or prescription drugs. Among younger students, inhalation of potentially lethal substances such as solvents and butane is more common than LSD use.

5

An LSD Distribution Network

Cynthia Favret

This chapter presents information about the workings and structure of an organized LSD sales and distribution network and the dealers and users who made up the network.[*] It is based on an interview with an undercover narcotics investigator who obtained an insider's view of the young men in the network, their operations, and their life-styles. Attention is given to the marketing and substance abuse practices that distinguish LSD dealers from dealers of other illegal substances (for example, cocaine and heroin). The intent of this study is threefold: (1) to determine how a particular LSD network was organized, managed, and linked to outside manufacturers/distributors; (2) to ascertain how LSD was obtained, distributed, and sold; and (3) to understand the behaviors, motivations, and life-styles of the individuals involved in the network.

Methods and Background

The author conducted an in-depth interview with a narcotics investigator working in a metropolitan area of the northeastern United States. The narcotics investigator and fellow officers were able to identify a local LSD distribution network. They obtained the neces-

---

[*] To honor assurances of confidentiality, the names of the community, the interviewee, and individuals identified by the interviewee are not revealed.

sary evidence to bring about legal charges and convictions of juveniles and adults, both locally and in several other cities.

The investigator had twelve years of experience in law enforcement (five in narcotics), involving undercover work as well as work
with a regional drug interdiction task force. The officer was identified by his supervisors as having direct and specialized experience
in LSD investigations. The interview was conducted at a district police station; it was taped and transcribed with controls applied to
maintain confidentiality. This report contains excerpts from the investigator's responses in the interview.

While LSD use is widely acknowledged by teenagers, it generally
goes undetected in a community until arrests bring it to the attention of the news media. Although numerous clinical studies have
been conducted on LSD during the past fifty years, relatively little
is known about the characteristics of current LSD users, how the
drug is introduced and established in a community, methods of
marketing and sales, and the social aspects or consequences of involvement in this particular drug culture.

This interview provides another perspective. It is a unique opportunity to obtain an understanding of the organization and
workings of a sizable LSD distribution network and its members.
Apprehension of LSD users typically occurs at low levels in a distribution network; rarely do police or drug enforcement officers obtain comprehensive information about the vertical structure of such
an operation. The following material provides some insight about
LSD distribution at several levels in one community.

Origin and Structure of the Network

The individual (referred to here as Alan) who organized and directed the network was a white male who was twenty two years old at
the time of his arrest. Alan began using marijuana at eleven or
twelve years of age and continued to use it throughout high school,
occasionally selling part of his supply to friends. Alan began dealing
marijuana on an organized basis after graduation from high school.
He very quickly learned how to transact business efficiently and
how to respond to market demands, produce the quality desired,
and identify his product.

He started out [as just a] nickel, dime pot dealer, selling $30, $40 of pot at a time. You can pick up a distributor for a couple ounces of pot anywhere; it's real easy, so he had no problem. He developed very quickly a knack for the business. . . . He saw all the money he could make very quick. He got very business-market valued. He knew if he got good marijuana instead of bad marijuana he could make more profit on it that way.

Alan became a fan of the Grateful Dead, a rock group established in the 1960s and known for its live concert performances. There are groups of fans who follow the Grateful Dead from city to city on their concert tours. These fans are often referred to as "Deadheads," and their lifestyle as "touring." During one of the tours, Alan encountered Harry (a pseudonym), a friend from high school. Harry had been touring for several years. He lived a marginal life-style, selling LSD to pay for his own drugs and to make enough money to live on. Harry eventually became an intermediary or middleman for the manufacturers.* In this role, he had access to large quantities of high-quality LSD.

When Harry told Alan that he could provide high-quality LSD on a regular basis, Alan realized the potential for profit. He quickly established a structure and hierarchy for LSD distribution. He would place an order with Harry and give a name and address for delivery. Harry then contacted his source in California, where the order was filled. When the source called Harry to confirm the delivery date, Alan sent Harry money for the LSD. Initially, Harry took his profit and forwarded the balance of the money to California. Over time, however, Harry's chronic use of LSD and other drugs eroded his ability to deal efficiently or profitably. As the network evolved, Alan began to send payment directly to California, with a small amount to Harry as a commission.

The LSD was typically sent via overnight delivery services; cash was usually sent through these services or a money-wiring service. Alan provided the addresses of young people, usually about eigh-

---

*During the investigation, it was learned that Harry had access to the inner circle of a large production and distribution network based in San Francisco. Information about manufacture and distribution at this level is largely anecdotal; individuals near this level have consistently refused to implicate their sources upon arrest.

teen years old, who had been told they could become important in his organization if they accepted packages.

> [Alan would say,] "Hey, accept this package for me and then I might consider letting you be one"—he'd call them lieutenants—"I'll let you be one of my lieutenants." . . . So he used that mentality to get people to accept packages for him, and they knew what they were and they wouldn't touch them. They were scared to death of him for it. . . . [Alan] would come over, and he'd give him the package and get nothing for it.

Alan interacted almost exclusively with a small number of mid-level dealers, most of whom he had known for some time. These mid-level dealers sold five to ten sheets (of one hundred hits each) of LSD and a pound or two of marijuana a week.

> The people they dealt with were eighteen, nineteen years old. Now, as it went down the chain, he was charged with distributing to juveniles because of the conspiracy theory. It finally got down to sixteen- and fifteen-, fourteen-, thirteen-year-old kids.

There were two groups of mid-level dealers, young white males aged nineteen to twenty-three whom Alan had known in high school. One group, composed of college students, will be referred to here as the "preppies." These young men were pursuing professional careers. Their primary motivation for selling LSD was to provide themselves with spending money and drugs for occasional recreational use. The other group lived marginal, dependent lifestyles; these young men lived with their parents and were consistently unemployed or worked sporadically. They will be referred to here as the "locals."

Alan's mid-level distributors sold LSD from sheets of one hundred hits each. Customers bought hits or single sheets. Alan's policy for the distribution network was to sell only to people known from school, and only when approached; sales were not actively solicited. Alan believed that by restricting sales to people they knew, they would never inadvertently sell to the police. In Alan's case, detection was in fact avoided for a relatively long period by this policy.

This distribution network was unusual in that people on the user level were aware of Alan's involvement. They knew his reputation and actively sought his drugs.

Oh, it was no big secret. Oh, it was well known where you could get [LSD] from. And unlike a lot of organizations [where] the people on the lower end don't know where it's coming from, everybody knew where this LSD was coming from. It was Alan's LSD. "I can't buy from Alan, [but] if I buy from [the local distributor], it's Alan's LSD."

The Participants

The Dealer

Alan took pride in his success as the largest dealer in the area and his reputation as a successful businessman who could be counted on to provide high-quality products. His primary product, and the one he preferred personally, was marijuana. He developed his LSD business because it was financially profitable, although he himself did not use it.

> Harry was a very big addict, all the time strung out, all the time tripping on acid, and Alan said, "Hey, that's not for me. I'm going to make the money off of it." And so what he did was, he just—the first time he went out, he picked up five sheets of LSD, which is five hundred hits, brought it back here and introduced it to the customers who use him for the marijuana, and it just took off. The price was right, the people liked what they got out of it. It was a lot what they call "cleaner" than what they had seen before.
>
> He then got real egotistical and he got into that "I'm the manager and I don't touch the stuff" and all, and he really liked to sit back and direct people. At that point he was getting sheets in for like $45 and selling them for $85, but he was basically trying to double his cost, double what he was putting out for it. And then he was using that money to help his reefer business because he really got into wanting to have everybody buying the reefer from him, so he kept dropping his [marijuana] price and dropping his price. And he got to a point where he really wasn't making a whole lot of money, so he was using his LSD business because he liked to be "the pot dealer" in this area.
>
> [He struck me like] the guy who has a hobby business and he goes out and he works for the government full time, and he takes a lot of his paychecks and he puts them into his fishing business or his sporting goods business, [which is] his real interest. And that reefer was his in-

terest and he had no wanting to deal with the LSD. He didn't like LSD, didn't like the people on LSD, but it supported his hobby.

Alan's success as a drug dealer was in sharp contrast with his prior endeavors. After graduation from high school, Alan continued to live with his mother and stepfather, reportedly unemployed and unable to hold a job for any length of time. He was described as disorganized and lazy, with no ambition or direction for his life. He drank daily. Drug dealing and the development of an identity as a successful purveyor of quality goods provided Alan with a focus.

He was very proud of himself, he was very—he felt very accomplished. This is the type of person that could never get a job. I mean, he just couldn't get up in the morning. He had no sense of responsibility, and I think this was something he succeeded in. He saw that he was succeeding, that he was making a lot of money. He basically built this business and he did a very nice job of it. He went out and he put things together; he managed his money well. . . . He had budgets for his trips. He did a real nice business management.

The narcotics investigator remarked on the difference between his personal life and his evolving identity as a businessman:

His life had no discipline. I mean, he came and went as he wanted to. He would not take care of his bills and stuff like that, but he always paid his source up [front] for the reefer. A guy down in [another state] who we identified and since arrested—paid him on time, all the time. His LSD was always paid in advance, which is a rarity that usually doesn't happen. . . . [He was] very business-minded, precise. Anybody he fronted dope to, he'd collect it—you know, "I'm giving you ten sheets of acid, I will pick up the money tomorrow at four o'clock," and at four o'clock he was there. He was always on time for a dope deal. I'm sure his whole life he never made other appointments, including probation appointments; he was late for those. . . . He was very proud of himself that he did such a good job.

Alan was able to maintain this disciplined approach to his business despite heavy use of alcohol.

Alan was an alcoholic, I guess. I don't know that much about the disease, but he drank constantly.

Vodka. He said that he's been drinking since he was ten years old. . . . Even once he was arrested, a lot of times I think that's why he wouldn't make probation [appointments], because he was hung over the next morning.

He did do some stupid things when he had been drinking. . . . Everybody always told me as the interviews went on. "We never dealt with Alan in the morning, you just cannot deal with him in the morning." And they kept saying it was hangover, but. . . . I think it was because he would drink in the morning and get that nice level before he could deal, and then he was able to function the rest of the evening.

In addition to being highly organized and attentive to detail in his drug dealing, Alan demonstrated a level of sophistication usually found only among people who deal cocaine or heroin on a large scale. He used rental cars during trips, carried false identification, and used other people to drive him back and forth. The narcotics investigator described his activities:

All the time changing drivers so that tickets didn't build up and he didn't get a history. He got people to rent cars, so he didn't have a history of renting cars. I mean, he was very intelligent in that point—to keep no paper trail behind him. Paid cash for everything, didn't stay at motels, didn't use gas credit cards [like] a lot of the American businessman dope dealers do.

Alan's self-esteem was intricately entwined with his success as an illicit entrepreneur and his need to have this image recognized and revered by others.

He thought that he was next to God. I mean, he just thought that everybody wanted to be like Alan. He said that many times, that everybody wanted to be like him.

The guy was so egotistical, he was just the easiest interview I had ever done.

Alan's approach to business was realistic and objective. He was aware of the risks involved, and he advised his distributors of those risks.

Again it was his business thing, it's part of the business. It's a risk you take when you get into the business, and he says that everybody knows it. And he, some of the other people that we arrested and interviewed later that cooperated said he told you when you got your business that, you know, "Here's how the business works, and there is risk involved, and if you get arrested . . . here's what you've got to do." He kind of laid both ends of it out for them.

Investigators were surprised that, upon his arrest, Alan identified so many members of his organization, including close friends and family members.

He gave up the whole organization. . . . He laid it all out, and again it was partly for his cooperation. He was going to get his sentence reduced from about twenty-two years to about ten years. . . . But I think his biggest motivation was [that] he was proud of what he did and he wanted to tell someone about it. You know how you interview people, you pick up what drives them and you kind of work that [in]to your interview. Well, every time he'd shut down on us, if we would say, "Hey, you're not going to get your deal," it's like you—what's ten or twenty-two years? But as soon as you started on his side and started saying, "I can't believe that you could put this deal together," then he just went off. For hours he would just set there, and I'd be steadily writing. Just so proud of how he put things together and had no qualms at all about giving up the whole [organization].

After he was arrested, Alan showed no remorse for his actions. Instead he was angry with his distributors, who had not conformed to his strict rules about dealing with outsiders not from school.

And that's how Alan was arrested. He was very bitter about it because, as he said, "I made no mistakes. I cannot control where that dope went. If the people under me had the same mentality I do or the same business sense . . . we wouldn't be in this particular status. It's their fault that I'm arrested." It was never his fault.

Alan appeared to feel that there was nothing inherently wrong with what he had done; the only problem was that he had been caught.

Even to the probation people, which is the person you . . . go in there and tell him, "I was wrong, I'm sorry, I'll never do it again." Alan told his probation people, "It ain't my fault that I got caught." Alan put it, "It ain't my fault I got arrested for this." That's his quote, and he never took responsibility for what he did.

If he told me once, he told me a hundred times, "If I had [it to do] all over again, I would do it, but I'd be much smarter the next time." No remorse.

Alan saw the failure to control his network as his only mistake. His anger was projected onto those who did not abide by the rules and, as a result, put him at risk. He focused his attention on assessing the damage to himself personally, assessing his current situation, and evaluating how best to extricate himself from his legal predicament.

The Distributors

Alan's distributors were of two distinct types. Although individuals in each of these groups sold similar amounts of the drug, their lifestyles, their motivation, and the efficiency of their operations were dramatically different. The preppies, who were for the most part academically successful in high school, continued to maintain high grades and run their businesses efficiently.

> They were all at college. Again, they had that mentality that they were making money, they needed money to live at college. They really didn't use the drug. . . . They looked at profit, they saved their money. They were the ones that kept turning it over, they knew when they would run out—they'd predict it, they kept records.

The locals sold LSD primarily to provide themselves with recreational drugs, social activity, and a minimal amount of spending money. Their dealings, in contrast with those of the preppies, were described as disorganized and haphazard, without concern for confidentiality, caution, or secrecy. All of the locals lived with their parents, although they maintained almost a boarder relationship with their families.

> It was weird, they were almost identical homes. Because the parents lived up on the top floor and the main living floor, and then there was a living room [den] in the basement that they had made a bedroom, and every one of these kids lived in the basement. I don't know why that happened to be, if it's just more privacy, whatever. It was nothing to go by their house at twelve or one o'clock in the afternoon to interview them and they'd be in bed still sleeping, food all over the floor. I mean,

just living like pigs. And you'd go upstairs, and it's a beautiful home with antiques and nice carpeting.

While the preppies were able to separate LSD dealing from the rest of their lives, the locals became increasingly absorbed in a lifestyle that consisted of partying, and they conducted their LSD distribution business casually. Of particular note is the distinction between these groups in terms of their direct involvement in using drugs. While the preppies used the drug occasionally, primarily at weekend parties, the locals maintained regular (and in several cases increased) use to the point of impairing their ability to conduct business.

It was kind of like [the] two split. This [distributor] who was his number one man was making straight As. . . . Just an excellent student, excellent parents, nice background, the whole bit—you'd never, ever think this kid's on dope. He used to deal ten sheets a week of LSD. On the other side, you had a lot of kids here that were nineteen, twenty, twenty-one, twenty-two years old, still living at home, never had a job since they graduated high school. Barely got through high school, just slugs, laying around sleeping all day long, partying all night. You know, they might go out and work for a day or two to get enough money to pay for a concert ticket, but other than that they weren't about to leave the house.

People that were using were bad dealers. Again, they didn't make any money, just laid around all day long.

Once you start seeing people using the drug, they are very bad distributors, very bad business people, whatever they happen to be selling.

Although both groups of distributors had similar access to Alan, the preppies established a closer business relationship because of his respect for their efficiency in managing the product and money. The organization was infiltrated by undercover police work through one of the locals. The investigator pointed out that if the local had not been so casual in his dealings, the organization probably would have continued without detection.

Unique Features of LSD Distribution

LSD is characteristically distributed by a person who identifies with the Grateful Dead rock group* and assumes a life-style somewhat reminiscent of the 1960s hippies or flower children. Immersion in this life-style is currently a common variable in LSD use and sale; becoming known among the Deadheads is often a prerequisite to engaging in any significant distribution of LSD.

> [LSD dealers are] completely different from anything else you deal with. Again, you usually have to tour with them. It's a lot of concerts and music, the Grateful Dead. They're a very hard group to get into, because before they deal . . . they want you to go to concerts with them. They want to come to your house and hang out, partying and all. . . . Cocaine people, most of them, once you get above a certain weight, it's very businesslike: "We don't want to know who you are." And LSD people are completely different. They want to know about you, they want to party with you, they want to hang out with you, they want to go away for the weekend up in the mountains, hiking with you. It's very much like the old '60s-type people. A lot of camping and hiking and sleeping-under-the-stars-type people, and most of the LSD people that deal use it quite heavily and they tour with the Dead, and it's not a business for them. It's, you know, I'll get five sheets, and I'll get them for $40 and I'll sell them for $45. I just need enough money, and that guy [Harry] who we were talking about earlier, that's what he did. He made just enough money to pay for his touring, but it wasn't a business to him.

> If you've got the mentality of traveling with the Dead and you don't mind living out of your car for a couple months, it would be very easy to break in. All you have to do is hang out with them for a while, and the way I understand it, it's not real hard. You don't need a lot of money because people will take care of you and they'll give you food, and all you've got to do is basically get with them and [be] willing to live the trashy life-style and you can just pick right up into it.

Mobile LSD conversion laboratories, where liquid or crystalline LSD is converted to edible forms, have been housed in recreational vehicles that tour with or follow the Grateful Dead. A local upsurge in LSD use often follows a Grateful Dead concert.

'Not all followers of the Grateful Dead are involved with LSD, nor has the band itself been implicated in LSD distribution.

We see fluctuations of LSD. Alan—there's very few of them in this area here. And what we see is, the Grateful Dead comes through or the Jerry Garcia concert comes through, and all of a sudden we'll see a lot of acid on the street and it will last for a couple of weeks and then it will go. And I think what's happening is, they go to the shows, they're not touring. Say somebody from [name of town] who used to know everybody, they're touring. The show comes into town, the local people who don't tour to go to the show, they hook up with this person, they get acid, enough that they can, whatever they can afford, a sheet or so, and [when] that last one is gone, it's gone.

The narcotics investigator noted distinct differences between those engaged in LSD use and distribution and dealers trafficking in drugs such as cocaine and heroin. Dealers of other drugs rarely sell LSD.

[LSD dealers] have a very open, "I don't give a damn" attitude. None of them have jobs, never want jobs. They don't think of things like getting a house and a family and a car. Cocaine people are very oriented towards money and material items. People that deal heroin, same way. It's a big money-making thing. Large amounts of reefer, it's a big money-making thing: I invest in assets, in money and gold jewelry. LSD dealers could care less. They don't want to make a lot of money. They just want enough money that they can live. They don't have to work. None of them, they don't have credit cards, they don't have jewelry. Cocaine people have more credit cards than we'd ever think about having. It's just a life, [a] free life-style.

I think a lot of people, if their primary motivation is money, they're going to pick one of the other drugs. And if they really want to sell LSD real bad, they maybe on the other hand don't want to live the lifestyle. . . . The Alans are few and far between out there.

LSD dealers make relatively little profit, except at the upper levels of production and distribution. Alan was able to obtain sheets of LSD for $45 and sell them to his distributors for $85; individual hits were sold for $3 or $4. It was possible, therefore, to make a 300 to 400 percent profit, but the sale of large numbers of individual hits is time-consuming. In comparison to other drugs, particularly cocaine, the profit margin is relatively small.

The people that are shipping it out of San Francisco are probably making at least a 300 percent or 400 percent increase if not more. . . . Once it gets to the sheet level, the profit margin drops.

Even if you're at the lab level, I don't think you can make the amount that you could with, say, cocaine or reefer. I mean, marijuana—you can go to Kentucky right now and buy it for $600 a pound. Bring it up here and sell it for $1,800 to $2,200 a pound. That's just over three times your profit margin very quickly. But I guess the big thing is, you're going for $600, you're making $1,200 on a deal. From there, if you take $500 worth of acid—that's a lot of acid—you turn it over, . . . you only make $1,000. It seems like much quicker, much easier to make it on cocaine and marijuana. A kilo [of cocaine] for $25,000 . . . turns into $300,000 by the time it gets to the street.

In addition to the comparatively low profit, the legal penalties for LSD distribution are severe.

It takes 100 grams of LSD to get you the mandatory twenty years, and cocaine, it would take about 50 kilos, I believe.

There was considerable naivete and simplicity of perspective among members of the network. While use of LSD was seen as a liberating recreational experience, use of other drugs such as heroin and cocaine had a negative connotation. People who used "hard" drugs were perceived as violent and alien to the LSD group. LSD use, in contrast, was not perceived as damaging, dangerous, or harmful. There was concern regarding the occasional bad trip, but LSD was generally regarded as a benign, "natural" substance.

[They felt that] anybody that deals heroin, "Oh, they're junkies, we don't want nothing to do with these people." They felt that LSD was fine. It was kind of like when you talk to people that deal reefer, it's a natural growth and therefore it's okay. Well, these people think that LSD is like a tranquilizer. It's a way to escape life for a short period and it's okay. There is nothing wrong with it, but if you do coke or you do heroin, you're really a freak of nature.

Several noted that driving under the influence of alcohol was a "real" public danger and commended police officers for intercepting these individuals.

If you went out and drove in the car drunk, that was really bad, but if you did some acid, that wasn't a big deal.

While there were political and cultural factors associated with LSD use in the era of hippies and flower children in the 1960s, the LSD users and distributors in this study did not particularly identify with these norms and values. A small subgroup of 1990s LSD users has adopted some of the accoutrements of the 1960s "age of enlightenment," such as tie-dyed shirts, long hair, beads, and sandals. Some of the youths were reluctant to eat synthetic or processed foods and preferred a vegetarian diet. The LSD distributors articulated a value system that included a general love of nature, the use of acid to heighten the appreciation and experience of the natural environment, and a belief in a "live and let live" ethos. There is no evidence of a common-interest literature (for example, the books of Carlos Castañeda or Herman Hesse, which some believe encouraged experimentation with drugs in the 1960s) or particular art or graphic style (such as the early 1960s psychedelia or pop art), or any religious/spiritual component to this life-style.

Families/Parents

The investigator was surprised that the highly unusual activities of the locals went seemingly unquestioned by many of their parents. The parents of the young men involved in distributing the LSD were in middle- and upper-middle-class socioeconomic groups. They tolerated and even supported behavior that essentially prolonged adolescence. The families were highly permissive, displaying a laissez-faire attitude toward the behavior of these young men. All the parents were surprisingly inattentive to obvious signs of drug activity.

Support for prolonged adolescence and a benign attitude toward behavior that would be alarming to others may reflect a perspective unique to some parents who grew up in the 1960s. The narcotics investigator speculated that perhaps prior exposure, experience, and opinions regarding drugs during their own adolescence may have influenced the desire and ability of these parents to manage the behavior of their children. Many of the parents appeared to avoid or to be afraid to confront their children about behaviors and activities. For example, shipments of the drug were often directed to the homes of users or friends of dealers via overnight delivery services.

> One guy's mom talked about these [overnight] packages that kept coming in every week. . . . They were usually U.S. mail overnight and they would come on Sunday, and she would leave them on the table for her son because they would come addressed to her son and he'd be eating breakfast. And I'd ask his mom, "Didn't you think it was strange that an eighteen-year-old would get [overnight packages]?" [She'd say,] "Well, we try to have an open relationship with our kids, and we didn't want to question him about it."

Alan lived with his mother and her second husband; his natural father was living in another state. The family was described as middle class, with two cars and a nice house. His parents knew that he was dealing, and in fact Alan's mother stored money for him in her room.

> When we did the search warrant that night, trying to be nice people . . . we only did his room and like common areas. We didn't want to go in the parents' room, thinking that they were the victim here. The mother had, I think it was $3,500, $4,500 of his. No, I'm sorry—it was more than that, it was $6,500 of his drug money in a box under her bed that she was storing for him.

Alan's stepfather, concerned about the drug activities, had told Alan that he "[did] not want anything in the house." He and Alan reportedly had "knock-down drag-out fights" about the drugs. The investigator indicated that the relationship between Alan and his mother was open, but unusual. He speculated she did not want to admit to herself that she knew her son's activities were illegal.

> It's that denial thing. . . . She did not want to admit that her son was dealing drugs. She liked the money, and he just flat out told her. He said, "She would have known anyways, so I might as well be honest with her." They had a kind of real wide-open relationship . . . [like] you probably strive to get with your own kids, but at the same time it was a strange relationship, where the things that he was allowed to do she did not mind. You know, he physically struck her. . . . When the undercover was there one time, he literally verbally abused his mother,

I mean, just strongly with very strong language, and she didn't mind that.

Impact on the Dealers, Their Families, and the Community

When Alan and members of his distribution network were arrested, they and their friends and families were shocked at the potential for serious legal consequences. Prosecution through the federal system mandates twenty years for 100 grams of LSD.

> They were shocked to find out that they could get—most of them were looking at twenty-four- to twenty-six-year sentences in the federal system. . . . In the state system they probably would have ended up with probation. I don't think any of them could have possibly gotten a day in jail. . . . They were shocked; they had no idea that they could get that much time in jail.

> Of course, once they got convicted they immediately went to jail, and it was a major shock to their parents. Their parents never thought it would end like this.

The narcotics investigator concluded that most of the young dealers were unaware of the consequences of a felony conviction.

> They were so shocked that they never got that far in their mind of that life-style. They were so worried about graduating college; quite a few of them were in college.

Only one, a preppie, seemed to realize that a felony conviction would severely restrict his life and career after release from prison. He was willing to plea bargain, preferring to plead guilty to a misdemeanor charge rather than risk the outcome of a felony trial. The arrests and convictions were a shock to the local youth community as well.

> I've been going to court for eleven years, the first one I've ever seen so many people come to a court case. . . . They were all high school kids. They were interested in what was going to happen, how the system worked, what these people were going to get, what was right, what was wrong. More than once at the breaks—because in the federal system the investigating officer sits up with the prosecuting attorney, so a lot of the

kids thought I was the prosecuting attorney—and when I would come out at the break in court, they would start asking me legal questions. Can you do this, can you do that, and I think it was a big education for them. It was all—this is a big game to them. And at this point they realized, "Hey, there is something wrong here, it is wrong." I'm sure that all their life they've heard these jail programs that say drugs are bad for you, etcetera, but this was like setting it in for them. . . . And even at the sentencing—nobody comes to the sentencing—there were probably the day that [the local distributor] got sentenced, there was fifty kids in the courtroom. Eighteen, nineteen, twenty-year-old kids.

Most of the individuals convicted were sentenced to long terms of incarceration. As the investigator pointed out, the legal consequences had an impact on the community:

In this one case, I think the penalties really struck home to these people that you can go to jail and go to real jail. It's not just getting arrested and getting out in an hour or whatever.

6

Legal Issues

Leigh A. Henderson

Detection

Until recently, LSD has been extremely difficult to detect in blood or urine, a factor that has contributed to its widespread use. LSD is used in quantities measured in micrograms and is almost completely metabolized; tests therefore must be able to detect nanogram and picogram amounts.* Simple and inexpensive screening tests for emergency room and forensic use have only recently become available and are rarely used.

Tests based on fluorescent spectroscopy and high-performance liquid chromatography (HPLC) were developed in the early 1970s. These tests were not very accurate, and they required large samples and a time-consuming process to extract the LSD.[53, 241] Radioimmunoassay (RIA) tests were developed about the same time.[242] These tests could detect as little as 20 pg/ml; they were inexpensive, simple to use, and required only small amounts of blood or urine. Early RIA tests were very good at detecting LSD when it was present in the blood or urine specimen. They produced positive results for some other substances as well, however, requiring that further tests be made.[241]

---

*1 nanogram (ng) = 1 billionth of a gram (10^9); 1 picogram (pg) = 1 trillionth of a gram (10^{-12}).

The United Kingdom's Forensic Service developed an improved RIA test that reacted only to LSD.[241] It detected levels as low as 3.0 ng/ml for urine and 1.2 ng/ml for blood. RIA tests are now commercially available and can detect even smaller quantities of the drug. One of these assays detects LSD in urine, whole blood or serum, and stomach contents at levels of 0.18, 0.05 to 0.06, and 0.18 ng/ml, respectively.[243]

Researchers in the United States have pursued the costlier and more time-consuming HPLC and gas chromatography-mass spectrometry (GC–MS) assays. The HPLC test was recently compared with RIA and was found to be less accurate.[244, 245] GC–MS can detect LSD at levels lower than the RIA (29 pg/ml in urine).[246] There is as yet no commercially available test using either of these assays, although research is continuing.[54, 247, 248]

Samples of LSD seized by law enforcement officials are similarly difficult to analyze. Some legal charges require only that the presence of LSD in the sample be demonstrated. The law in federal and some state courts, however, imposes penalties based on the amount of LSD involved. GC-MS tests can determine whether a sample contains LSD, but not the amount. A technique called circular dichroism spectropolarimetry can be used to measure the amount of LSD in drug samples.[249]

Legal Penalties

State penalties for possession or distribution of LSD vary widely (Table 8) and change from time to time. For possession of LSD, the maximum sentence for a first offense ranges from thirty days (Wisconsin) to life imprisonment (Texas). Some states include LSD with narcotics and cocaine as drugs that are targeted for stricter penalties. These states impose heavier penalties, usually based on the amount of LSD involved.[250]

Most states have additional laws that may be applied in drug-related cases; these include provisions about drug sales to juveniles and sales in or around schools. Measures against drug paraphernalia and precursor chemicals also can be applied in LSD cases. In addition to fines, some states seize drug dealers' assets and apply taxes on profits from the sale of controlled substances.[250] Other legal measures may be invoked for individuals convicted of drug offens-

TABLE 8

*State Controlled Substances Acts: Comparison of Penalties for
Possession and Manufacture/Delivery/Sale of LSD
(First Offense), 1991*

State	Possession Years in Jail	Possession Fine ($)	Manufacture/Delivery/Sale Years in Jail	Manufacture/Delivery/Sale Fine ($)	Additional Penalty as a Targeted Substance
Alabama	1–10	5,000	2–20	10,000	Based on amount
Alaska	0–5	50,000	0–10	50,000	
Arizona	0–5	1,000–150,000	5.5–14	1,000–150,000	
Arkansas	3–10	10,000	5–40	15,000	
California	0–1		2–4		
Colorado	4–16	3,000–750,000	4–16	3,000–750,000	
Connecticut	0–1	1,000	0–7	25,000	Based on amount
Delaware	0–6 mos.	1,000	0–5	1,000–10,000	Based on amount
District of Columbia	0–1	1,000	20 mos.–5yrs.	50,000	
Florida	0–5	5,000	0–5	5,000	
Georgia	2–15		5–30		
Hawaii	0–20	10,000–50,000	0–20	25,000–50,000	
Idaho	0–1	1,000	0–5	15,000	Higher base penalty
Illinois	1–3	15,000	2–30	150,000–500,000	Based on amount
Indiana	1–5	10,000	10	10,000	
Iowa	0–1	1,000	0–10	1,000–50,000	Based on amount
Kansas	0–1	2,500	3–life	300,000	Based on amount
Kentucky	1–5	3,000–5,000	1–5	3,000–5,000	
Louisiana	0–10	5,000	5–30	15,000	
Maine	0–1	1,000	0–10	2,500–10,000	Based on amount
Maryland	0–4	25,000	0–5	15,000	Based on amount
Massachusetts	0–1	1,000	0–10	1,000–10,000	
Michigan	0–1	1,000	0–7	5,000	
Minnesota	0–5	10,000	0–15	100,000	
Mississippi	0–3	1,000–30,000	0–30	1,000–1,000,000	
Missouri	0–7	5,000	5–15	5,000	Based on amount

TABLE 8 *Continued*

State	Possession		Manufacture/Delivery/Sale		Additional Penalty as a Targeted Substance
	Years in Jail	Fine ($)	Years in Jail	Fine ($)	
Montana	0–5	50,000	1–life	50,000	
Nebraska	0–5	10,000	0–50	25,000	
Nevada	1–6	5,000	1–20 or life	20,000	
New Hampshire	0–7	25,000	0–7	100,000	Based on amount, with higher base
New Jersey	3–5	25,000	3–5	15,000	Based on amount
New Mexico	0–1	500–1,000	0–3	5,000	
New York	0–1	1,000	0–7	5,000	
North Carolina	0–5	5,000	0–10	fine	Based on amount
North Dakota	0–5	5,000	0–10	10,000	Based on amount
Ohio	1.5–5	2,500	1–15	2,000–7,500	
Oklahoma	2–10		2–life	20,000	Based on amount
Oregon	0–10	100,000	0–20	100,000	
Pennsylvania	0–1	5,000	0–5	15,000	
Rhode Island	0–3	5,000	0–life	100,000–500,000	Based on amount
South Carolina	0–6 mos.	1,000	0–5	5,000	
South Dakota	0–5	5,000	1–10	10,000	
Tennessee	0–1	2,500	8–30	100,000	Based on amount
Texas	2–life	10,000–100,000	5–life	20,000–250,000	
Utah	0–5	5,000	1–15	15,000	
Vermont	0–20	500,000	0–20	500,000–1,000,000	
Virginia	1–10	1,000	5–40	100,000	
Washington	0–5	10,000	0–5	10,000	
West Virginia	90 days–6 mos.	1,000	1–5	15,000	
Wisconsin	0–30 days	500	0–5	15,000	Based on amount
Wyoming	0–6 mos.	750	0–10	10,000	

Source: National Criminal Justice Association, 1991.

es. Drivers' licenses may be revoked, and professional licenses in education, child care, health, or other professions providing services to minors may be refused, suspended, or revoked by the respective licensing boards.

In federal law, the possession, manufacture, and distribution of LSD is penalized under the section of the federal code for nonnarcotic Schedule I drugs. The penalty for simple possession of LSD is a maximum of one year in prison and/or a minimum fine of $1,000 for the first offense. The penalty increases for subsequent offenses to a mandatory three months to three years in prison and/or a minimum fine of $5,000.[250]

In federal law, LSD is a targeted substance with mandatory minimum penalties (Table 9). Penalties for manufacture and distribution of targeted substances depend on the amount of drug involved, the number of previous offenses, and whether or not the offender is acting in partnership. (They also take into account a buyer's death or serious injury, clauses unlikely to be required for LSD sales.) For amounts of LSD of 1 to 10 grams, the base penalty is five to forty

TABLE 9

Federal Controlled Substances Act: Penalties for Manufacture, Delivery, or Sale of LSD, 1991

	Base Penalty		If Death or Serious Injury Results from Use
Offense	Years in Jail	Fine ($)	Years in Jail
Between 1 and 10 grams			
First offense	5–40	2 million	20–life
Second offense	10–life	4 million	life
Subsequent offenses	life	8 million	
More than 10 grams			
First offense	10–life	4 million	20–life
Second offense	20–life	8 million	life
Subsequent offenses	life	8 million	

Source: National Criminal Justice Association, 1991.

years in prison and a fine of up to $1 million. For amounts of LSD of 10 grams or more, the base penalty is ten years to life in prison and a fine of up to $4 million. These base penalties escalate for subsequent offenses and are greater if a group rather than an individual is involved.[250]

A Supreme Court ruling in 1991 has had a profound impact on sentencing for LSD-related offenses. Federal law stipulates that the amount of drug involved is the weight of "a mixture or substance containing a detectable amount" of the drug. Cocaine and heroin are often diluted with look-alike substances to increase the dealer's profits. This vehicle is sold as cocaine or heroin. The most common vehicle for LSD, blotting paper, neither dilutes the drug nor increases profit. The inclusion of the weight of the blotting paper as part of the weight of the LSD sold was challenged in the Supreme Court, but the Court ruled that the weight of the paper should be included in determining penalties.[107] This has resulted in lengthy federal sentences for LSD distribution. In California, one youth was sentenced to fifteen years and eight months in federal prison for three grams of LSD carried on 440 grams of blotting paper.[251] In Arizona, another youth was sentenced to a minimum of ten years for involvement in the sale of 1.5 grams of LSD on 100 grams of blotting paper.[252]

To put this in perspective, consider 10 grams of LSD and five kilos of powdered cocaine—the amounts mandating a federal ten-year sentence. Using the DEA's standard dosage unit for LSD of 50 micrograms, 10 grams of pure LSD would equal some two thousand doses, with a street value of about $600,000. The wholesale price of 5 kilos of cocaine in 1990 was $65,000 to $200,000; after being cut and resold multiple times, the street value would be many times higher. If the law was meant to target LSD dealers on that scale, its application appears to be producing quite different an effect. Ten grams is the approximate weight of thirty sheets of blotter paper. Thirty sheets of LSD paper contain three thousand doses, or 0.15 gram of LSD, with a street value of $9,000 (still an amount beyond any need for "personal use").

Despite the heavy federal penalties, LSD arrests and seizures are comparatively few. In 1991, slightly more than 1 percent of the total DEA drug arrests (205 out of nearly 17,000 arrests) involved LSD. This was a slight increase from 1990 (103 out of 23,000, or

0.4 percent). Arrests and seizures of various drugs are heavily dependent on the allocation of resources made by the DEA. After several years of falling numbers of LSD arrests and seizures, the DEA in 1990 allocated additional resources for LSD investigations, and these numbers again began to climb. Class 1 and 2 felony arrests involving LSD averaged thirty-five a year between 1986 and 1988, fell to nineteen in 1989, and climbed to thirty-two and eighty-five in 1990 and 1991, respectively. During 1990, about five hundred thousand dosage units of LSD were confiscated by the DEA. The last major seizure of laboratories producing LSD occurred in the state of Washington in 1981.[107]

7

Summary and Implications

William J. Glass

Leigh A. Henderson

Cynthia Favret

The basis of illicit LSD use has changed little over the past thirty years, if we accept the testimonials of the adolescents and parents interviewed for this book. As they describe, most use begins when experienced users introduce friends and acquaintances to what they consider initially a safe and fun experience. Today's LSD doses are considerably smaller (per unit) than in the 1960s. Yet hits of acid work on groups of youngsters much the same way in the 1990s as in past generations. To a large extent, LSD use today occurs in much the same groups, albeit younger, and for many of the same reasons as at any time in the past thirty years.

From the qualitative and quantitative data we have presented, a picture of LSD use and its consequences emerges. It is hoped that this snapshot of the nature and extent of contemporary LSD use helps readers understand and appreciate the facts most often obscured in the occasional sensational popular media exposure LSD receives. Among the facts most often overlooked are these findings:

- LSD use is relatively uncommon in comparison with use of alcohol, marijuana, or cocaine and misuse of prescription drugs.
- Adverse health consequences of LSD are comparatively rare, with "bad trips" being the most common adverse reaction.
- Although some health consequences may be related to length of

use, size of dose, and the interaction of other drugs, there is considerable uncertainty over why LSD adversely affects some individuals more severely than others.

- Long-term trends in LSD use show stability over the last fifteen years in both proportion and age of users.
- LSD is primarily used by suburban white males in their late teens and early 20s. A shift in use from the upper level of this band to the lower level could contribute to the perception that use has increased among young adolescents.
- LSD is characterized by infrequent episodic use culminating in "maturing out" after two to four years.

When viewed in the context of drug use among the population as a whole, or among drug users in general, LSD use is comparatively rare. The drug seems to appeal to a limited group of adolescents and an even smaller group of older persons who may still seek to identify with a particular subculture. LSD is used less frequently among high school students than alcohol, marijuana, or (for recreational use) over-the-counter or prescription drugs. Currently use among high school students is about as frequent as that of cocaine. Among younger students, inhalation of potentially lethal substances such as solvents and butane exceeds LSD use.

The typical LSD user differs from a typical user of drugs such as opiates in that LSD appeals to individuals who are often socioeconomically advantaged, who have the opportunity for higher education and successful careers, yet who choose—at least for a time—not to follow societal norms. Some factors preceding adolescent drug use in general include low self-esteem, rebelliousness, depression, aggressiveness, perhaps shyness, a lack of norms, and poor academic performance—a syndrome of problem behavior of which drug use is a part rather than a determinant.[239, 253–254] Other characteristics linked to adolescent substance abuse include peer influence, involvement in other delinquent activities, an adolescent's own beliefs and values, and parental drug use, values, and relationships.[239] Although these factors may predispose to drug use, they do not explain the specific appeal of LSD to suburban youth.

As the authors of Chapter 1 note, the adolescent users interviewed agreed that they used LSD because it was fun and because they were bored. They said they took LSD to add interest to otherwise mundane events and activities. As a drug that tends to promote introspection and to heighten the senses, it has more to offer those in relatively safe and pleasant surroundings than those in the more dangerous and unpleasant inner-city environment. In fact, the suburban youths interviewed seemed to take LSD as a controlled means of losing control. Riding a roller coaster may be an appropriate analogy; the ride is safe, but contains enough sense of danger to be thrilling.

In studies of young adults in the 1960s and 1970s, LSD users emerge as intelligent underachievers. The use of psychedelic drugs was associated with discontentment with oneself, the desire and willingness to change, disenchantment with society, alienation from its values, pessimism about the future, and an inability to communicate with parents. Users felt a lack of control over their lives, and they were hostile to authority figures and external agencies they perceived as having this control. These traits appeared to precede, rather than result from, psychedelic use.[255, 256] More recently, hallucinogen use among adolescent boys was found to be significantly higher in those who were shy and yet felt a strong need to be with other people.[257]

Reasons for choosing the drug LSD were detailed in a classic article a quarter of a century ago.[60] First, LSD yields an intense experience without clouding of consciousness. The drug has a compelling immediacy; the flood of perceptions demands attention to the present. Users often laugh or cry in an apparent release of tension in response to the drug. Some users seem motivated by desire for the intensification of mood and emotions that LSD can give.

Others choose LSD because of the group aspect of the drug. A good LSD experience demands that the environment provide structure and support. Taking LSD with a group of good friends or an older, more experienced "guide" can ensure that the trip is enjoyable, and the group or guide can provide support if the user begins to feel panic or anxiety. For others, using LSD provides camaraderie; it is a ticket to membership in a group—the need for sociability noted above.

Finally, some users choose LSD as an emotional fitness test. There is always the inner threat of loss of control, and some users feel it important to confront and conquer this threat from within themselves. Others seem to be rehearsing the strength and autonomy that will be demanded from them as adults. They are probing and testing the consequences of making their own decisions.

Some motivations for using LSD, however, appear to have changed over the years. The explosion of LSD use in the 1960s took place among relatively affluent college-age youth dissatisfied with the status quo. They became interested in alternatives to materialism and in increased self-knowledge. LSD was used to expand consciousness, to explore the mind, and as a hallmark of particular political attitudes. Users in the 1990s report taking LSD for its visual effects and its ability to enhance such pleasurable but ordinary experiences as hiking or watching movies. The use of LSD is less tied to a particular subculture than it was in the 1960s and 1970s; the distinction between those who are straight and those who are hip seems less pronounced. At least according to the LSD users interviewed here, high school users of LSD are drawn from all social subgroups, from jocks to preppies to cheerleaders and straight-A students. The search for cosmic enlightenment and mystical experience that motivated some LSD users in the 1960s is seldom mentioned today. It is not known if this difference is dose related.

LSD has several attributes that contribute to its popularity among adolescents. It has no color, odor, or taste, and it is very easy to conceal (a million 50-microgram doses of LSD weigh only about two ounces). LSD is inexpensive, costing users some three to five dollars per "hit" (dose). Tests have been unable to detect LSD in blood or urine for much of its history as a street drug; although tests are now commercially available, they are expensive, time-consuming, and seldom used. As a result, difficulty in detecting LSD use is likely to be a factor that encourages its use. Finally, the adolescent users perceived the drug as not particularly harmful and even as "organic"—innately benign because it occurred naturally. They tended to look down on users of "dangerous" drugs such as heroin and cocaine.

LSD use has increased slightly over the past several years, but evidence of a current nationwide epidemic is not compelling. Although local outbreaks of LSD use are periodically reported in communities across the United States, other communities report none. Significant increases in LSD supplies have not been reported at the national level in recent years. Evidence generally does not support the popular idea that an LSD epidemic is now occurring, or that one can be expected in the near future.

National surveys are limited, however, in that they are unable to reflect local fluctuations in LSD use. These have been reported in association with concert tours of certain rock music bands, and they may occur for other reasons as well. These sporadic "local outbreaks" of LSD use experienced by communities throughout the country are likely to continue. In fact, they seem to be characteristic of the drug. In a study written in 1965, it was noted that the supply of hallucinogens seemed to fluctuate much more than supplies of narcotics or amphetamines and barbiturates.[258] Several reasons for this phenomenon were proposed, all of which seem equally valid today. First, it was suggested, demand is more erratic because the hallucinogens are not addictive, and fewer people want to use them on a regular basis. Second, many fewer people use these drugs than engage in the illicit use of amphetamines and barbiturates. Unlike hallucinogens, the latter drugs are available by prescription and consequently are accessible (licitly or illicitly) to more people. Finally, it was noted, hallucinogens do not present the great financial incentive presented by narcotics (and now cocaine).

The perception of increased LSD use may be encouraged by factors other than a real increase in the number of people using it. The general lack of evidence to support the popular perception that LSD use is spreading suggests that other explanations for the persistence of these perceptions should be considered. For example, increased media attention may play a role. In the 1980s, news stories centered on intravenous drug use (because of its connection with AIDS) and on the devastating effects of the crack cocaine epidemic; the media may perceive the public as ready for a new type of drug story. The generation that first encountered LSD now has children who are old enough to be vulnerable to drug use. Many are surprised to learn that LSD is still very much part of the array of illicit drugs available, and provide a ready audience for stories about LSD's supposed resurgence.

Alternatively, the age distribution of LSD use may have shifted. LSD was used mainly by college students in the 1960s and 1970s; its use may be more visible if current users are younger and subject to closer monitoring by parents and teachers. The data, however, do not conclusively support an increase in the number of younger users. This question, of paramount concern to parents and educators, is difficult to answer with certainty in the absence of historical comparisons. Data are largely anecdotal; they have not been routinely collected on children younger than high school seniors. Even current data on drug use among middle or elementary school children are inadequate. The adolescents interviewed for this book had begun LSD use at age twelve. The data available indicate that use at this very young age is not new, but has occurred throughout the last fifteen years.

Several possible explanations exist for the perception that LSD users in the 1990s are younger than in previous decades. First, the age range for greatest susceptibility (seventeen to twenty) includes both high school and college-age students. It is possible that initiation within that age range has shifted to students in the high school rather than the college environment. Second, the lower limit of the range of ages at initiation may have become lower without significantly affecting the median. There are indications from several sources that such a shift may have occurred in the early 1980s; unfortunately, this hypothesis is not directly testable using the available data sources. Finally, the perception may be at least partially just that—a perception not supported by fact. When LSD was legal in the first part of the 1960s, it attracted a great deal of popular press. Writers such as Tom Wolfe and Ken Kesey tended to write about their contemporaries, who were well educated and certainly not of high school age. The existence of the youngest LSD users may simply have escaped publicity.

Whether or not use is increasing overall, regional fluctuations in supply and demand are likely to continue to cause alarm in the communities in which they occur. LSD is one of the most potent of all illicit drugs in that a minute amount produces profound effects. It is only natural to expect that such a powerful drug must have equally powerful consequences to physical and mental health. Yet direct health consequences associated with LSD use are minimal in comparison with those of other illicit drugs.

Additional biomedical research is a prerequisite to explaining LSD's mechanism of action and its biologic effects. LSD has not, however, been found to cause organic damage, chromosomal damage, cancer, or birth defects. It is not particularly toxic; in the medical literature only two deaths have been attributed to an overdose of LSD. In both these cases, evidence was largely circumstantial rather than forensic. Although LSD creates tolerance, it is not addictive, in that there is no LSD withdrawal syndrome. Apart from occasional lethargy (due perhaps to lack of sleep), it causes no hangover. Viewed strictly in the context of traditional drug-induced health consequences (measured in injury and death), LSD is less dangerous than most other illegal drugs. Use by adolescents, however, carries additional risks to psychologic maturation and academic performance much the same as do marijuana and other drugs typically used at this stage in life.

The serious adverse effects popularly attributed to LSD—irrational acts leading to suicide, accidental death, or other physical harm—are extremely rare. Contributing factors are usually overlooked. Specifically, two conditions exist that may predispose an individual to a higher risk of an adverse reaction to LSD: a preexisting psychiatric disorder, and the use of other drugs in conjunction with LSD. Frequently these conditions coexist, and in these specific instances LSD may precipitate a more prolonged or severe psychotic reaction. Certainly the use of LSD should signal intense concern when it is part of a broader pattern of drug use, or when an individual has an underlying psychiatric problem. The threat of genetic or organic damage caused by LSD, however, is minimal if any.

Panic reactions (bad trips) may be severe enough in inexperienced users to result in a trip to an emergency room or crisis intervention center. These episodes resolve quickly, though, when the drug is metabolized. More experienced users will "talk down" friends who have a bad trip. Users in this and other studies report accepting these episodes as part of the experience, much as drinkers expect an occasional hangover. Bad trips are usually not seen as a reason to avoid using LSD among those whose use persists beyond one or two episodes.

The LSD user in the 1990s has, at least nominally, a greater degree of control over his or her trip than did previous users. Typical doses are much lower than those taken in earlier decades. The average dose of "blotter acid" commonly available today ranges between 20 and 80 micrograms (some two to twelve times lower than the average dose in the 1960s). At lower doses, LSD's perceptual effects are dominant. The emotional and psychic effects sought by 1960s users require higher doses and present a higher risk of experiencing a bad trip.

These lower doses have probably contributed to the decline in bad trips seen at emergency rooms. The lower doses are strong enough to produce the characteristic perceptual effects of LSD, but they can produce the psychic effects only if multiple hits are consumed. A user, however, can never be certain of the amount of LSD that is taken. The dosage can be affected by the manufacturing technique, the delivery medium, the time since manufacture, and storage conditions.

Generations of LSD users have developed and perpetuated a body of popular knowledge about the drug. LSD users recognize that, far more than for other drugs, the effects of LSD vary with the setting, mood, and expectations of the user. Most try to plan their trips to avoid situations that place them in danger. Control of the dosage, the setting, use of other drugs, companions, and other external events and stimuli significantly reduce the risk of a bad experience. Many experienced users do not trip alone. While for some a shared LSD experience is an opportunity for bonding with peers, others prefer to trip in a group in case someone requires help on a bad trip.

According to the LSD users interviewed in this study, frequent ingestion of LSD over a period of several months to several years can lead to social and personal disintegration. School performance declines, personal hygiene is neglected, and attention to sleep and nutrition lapses. Over time, chronic users increasingly lose control of their lives. As parents and drug abuse treatment counselors can attest, this pattern is not unique to LSD users, and rarely does LSD use precede or preclude use of alcohol, marijuana, and other drugs. In fact, most LSD users are likely to be using other substances, including alcohol, and the effects of LSD may be difficult to distinguish from problems associated with multiple substance abuse.

The users interviewed here also used other drugs (one had entered treatment after an episode in which he took seventeen nighttime cold capsules), yet they all attributed their personal declines to LSD. The attribution of substance abuse problems to LSD, regardless of other contributing factors, can be observed in the medical literature. It occurs among not only patients and parents bringing their children for treatment but physicians and researchers as well. The label *LSD user* may be applied to distinguish a person who uses LSD from a person who does not, even when both use other drugs as well.

LSD distribution appears to be loosely structured, particularly at the lowest "retail" levels, and to differ from that of heroin and cocaine. "Business" dealings tend to be friendly and based on personal acquaintance rather than financial gain. While profit was a motive for the distributor described in Chapter 5 and for his college-based dealers, it was the other group of dealers that seemed to be more typical. These individuals sold just enough LSD to maintain themselves in a marginal life-style.

LSD seems not to be "pushed" as other drugs are. The dealers in Chapter 5 sold to personal acquaintances in order to avoid detection; they waited to be approached rather than seeking out new users. The adolescents interviewed here denied that they were influenced by peer pressure, although the adults perceived the situation differently. Different conceptions of "peer pressure" appear to be used by parents and children. To the adults, LSD was introduced by outsiders who were only pretending to be friends. To the youngsters, LSD was available; they knew where to get it if they wanted it. While using it was often a group activity, they did not feel that they were coerced into using LSD.

The interviews in Chapter 1 and the documentation of the LSD distribution network in Chapter 5 provide some compelling indicators for potential prevention or intervention. If it can be assumed that these groups of young people are representative of current youth culture, some hypotheses about their perceptions of LSD use can be advanced.

While LSD is perceived by older adults, law enforcement, and the courts as a dangerous drug, many young people see it as largely harmless or benign. To them, using LSD is a recreational activity to be enjoyed in a social context. LSD is unique in that regard—in contrast with drugs such as heroin, cocaine, and sometimes alcohol, which are largely regarded by these youths as addictive and harmful to both the user and to society.

The young people were shocked when confronted with the serious legal penalties for LSD distribution. Both parents and children had difficulty accepting the reality of the legal consequences. The narcotics investigator noted that even as the individuals were led away in handcuffs by federal marshals, families seemed unable to comprehend the long-term consequences. Because of the lengthy sentences and the felony convictions, graduation or a professional career was essentially out of the question for these young people.

An effective intervention or prevention strategy to help curb LSD distribution and use may lie in increasing awareness of the potential harsh legal consequences of LSD distribution and their impact on plans for even the short-term future. The noncommercial social philosophy of the environment surrounding LSD use and sales makes it difficult for young people to view LSD as a dangerous drug. Although it is too soon to assess the lasting impact, awareness of the legal consequences of distribution seems to have had a profound effect on the community whose experiences are presented here, particularly on those who observed the legal process through the sentencing phase.

Effective prevention may include increasing adolescents' awareness of the federal penalties when conspiracy convictions are pursued, as opposed to the generally more lenient statutory sentencing guidelines. The impact of federal versus state sentencing is even more significant in light of the interpretation of federal sentencing guidelines that specify weight of seized LSD to be determined on the basis of total weight, including the carrier or medium on which the drug is sprayed or applied. In the case of LSD, this carrier is paper when the drug is processed and sold in sheets, its most common street form. The weight of the carrier paper is likely to increase the total weight to more than 10 grams for even a small amount of LSD. As noted in Chapter 6, first-time offenders convicted of possessing amounts in excess of 10 grams face a federal sentence range of ten years to life. Legal penalties of this severity are far beyond the expectations of the majority of casual users, and dissemination of this information may be an effective deterrent for some.

Similarly, a certain segment of the recreational user population may be influenced by education regarding the impact of a felony conviction on future career options. While most college-bound or motivated youth anticipate professional achievement, many are unaware that a felony conviction virtually denies them access to many professions, including many of those requiring licensure by a state board (medicine, dentistry, psychology, law) or clearance for government or security jobs. This would clearly represent more of an obstacle, and thus more of a deterrent, to the college-oriented sub-group of users than to those who are more vested in the Deadhead life-style, which eschews traditional material achievement.

Facing problems in the family setting early enough to effect a successful resolution is a lesson that some may draw from the pro-files in this report. Drug abuse prevention messages that emphasize parental involvement in the process of maturation from childhood through adolescence to adulthood have not succeeded for the young people described here. Poor communication between parent and child is one of the factors most associated with use of illicit drugs. Parents need to realize that LSD use is difficult to detect and can occur in any home.

One of the major shortcomings of drug use prevention efforts has been the lack of credibility. Adolescents today are not as naive about drugs as adults might believe. Many are well-informed about drugs, either through experimentation or observation. Some seek out material from the popular and scientific press in an attempt to learn more about drugs and their effects. Exaggerated claims about the negative effects of LSD or any drug can only discredit the factu-al material presented. Such claims will only reinforce a belief held by youngsters that authority figures do not provide accurate or reli-able information. Adults cannot present accurate information, however, if they themselves do not have it. It is hoped that through efforts such as this book, adults in contact with youths making de-cisions about LSD and other drugs will be better able to provide in-formation that maintains credibility while effectively discouraging use. Persuasion will be most effective when messages neither distort nor exaggerate LSD's negative characteristics.

LSD, however, is only one of many drugs to which today's ado-lescents will be exposed. If we hope to teach and communicate pre-vention information to our children, they and we both must be knowledgeable about drugs like LSD. Accurate and reliable infor-mation about LSD should continue to be part of a broader program of drug information provided to adolescents. LSD use should be considered as part of a pattern of drug use (or at least drug knowl-edge) beginning in junior high or even elementary school.

Concern about LSD should not displace concern about use of other drugs, including alcohol and tobacco. Not only are their detrimental effects and risks to health well-documented, but use of these substances is exceptionally widespread. Alcohol as a drug used by adolescents deserves more attention than it has so far received. (Inhalants, too, deserve special mention as extremely hazardous drugs. The vapors of literally hundreds of substances can be inhaled. Many impede the flow of oxygen to the brain, and can result in permanent severe damage or death.)

We hope to encourage other researchers to adopt and develop the approach we have used. Researchers often succumb to a debate over the merits of quantitative versus qualitative data. We believe there are tremendous advantages in using both. As science has gained control over some of the plagues of mankind, we are left with afflictions that often contain a major behavioral component— cancer and heart disease, sexually transmitted diseases, and of course drug use. Without an understanding of *why* people use certain drugs, *how* they use drugs, and the *consequences* of drug use, we cannot hope to influence changes in behavior. Without knowledge of *who* uses drugs and how many people are affected, effective planning for prevention cannot occur.

Appendix:
Major Data Sources

National Household Survey on Drug Abuse

The National Household Survey on Drug Abuse[7] (NHSDA, or Household Survey) is a series of studies designed to measure the prevalence of alcohol, tobacco, and drug use in the United States and to monitor trends in use over time. The first two surveys, conducted in 1971 and 1972, were sponsored by the National Commission on Marihuana and Drug Abuse. Later surveys were conducted periodically (in 1974, 1976, 1977, 1979, 1982, 1985, 1988, and 1990) and sponsored by the National Institute on Drug Abuse (NIDA). Since 1990, the survey has been conducted annually. Responsibility for the survey was transferred in 1992 from NIDA to the newly created Substance Abuse and Mental Health Services Administration (SAMHSA).

NHSDA is a representative sample of the household population of the United States aged twelve and older (Alaska and Hawaii were included for the first time in 1991). The sample design is a multistage area probability sample. To increase the reliability of estimates, population groups of special interest have been oversampled. People under age thirty-five have always been oversampled, and black and Hispanic households have been oversampled since 1985. In 1990 the Washington, D.C., metropolitan statistical area (MSA) was oversampled, and in 1991 five other MSAs were oversampled as well: Chicago, Denver, Los Angeles, Miami, and New York. Civilians living on military bases and persons living in noninstitutional group quarters (college dormitories, rooming houses, and shelters) were excluded until 1991.

NHSDA respondents are interviewed in their homes by trained interviewers. Respondents mark answer sheets in response to questions either read aloud by the interviewer or, in the case of illicit drug use, printed on cards. Respondents are assured of anonymity, and interviewers do not see the completed answer sheets.

NHSDA provides nationwide and regional prevalence data for alcohol, drug, and tobacco use. Estimates are presented for use in the respondent's lifetime, in the past month (the month before the survey), and in the past year (the year before the survey). The survey is valuable because it measures the extent of drug use in the largest part of the population (estimated to be more than 98 percent of the total). The subpopulations excluded are homeless persons, persons living in correctional facilities, nursing homes, and treatment centers, and active military personnel. If drug use in these groups differs from that of the larger population, the NHSDA may provide slightly inaccurate estimates of drug use in the total population. Drugs that are rarely used, such as heroin, are more likely to be affected by such inaccuracies.

Monitoring the Future (High School Senior Survey)

Monitoring the Future[6,8] is designed to characterize substance use, trends, attitudes, and beliefs. It is a long-term research program conducted at the University of Michigan's Institute for Social Research under a series of research grants from NIDA. It consists of an annual survey of high school seniors, conducted since 1975, as well as annual follow-up surveys of representative samples of previous participants. This provides information on drug use among young adults, both in and out of college. Younger students (from the eighth and tenth grades) were included beginning in 1991.

The annual sample is selected in a multistage random sampling procedure of high schools within geographic areas. The survey is administered in classrooms during a normal class period whenever possible, although in some schools a larger group administration is required. The follow-up sample consists of a representative sample of 2,400 individuals selected from the 15,000 to 17,000 participating in a given class. To ensure reliability of estimates, heavier users are oversampled. These respondents are assigned to one of two groups and surveyed by mailed questionnaire—one group in even-numbered calendar years, and the other in odd-numbered calendar years.

Monitoring the Future provides nationwide and regional prevalence data for alcohol, drug, and tobacco use. Estimates are presented for use in the respondent's lifetime, in the past month (the month before the survey), and in the past year (the year before the survey). It also surveys attitudes and beliefs about various substances.

This survey does not include school dropouts or persons who were absent the day the questionnaire was given. Dropouts and youths who are frequently absent, however, are more likely to use drugs than students in school. About 15 to 20 percent of each entering class will drop out before finishing high school, so the survey probably underestimates total drug use among school-aged youths.

Both the Household Survey and *Monitoring the Future* canvas the population that is believed, on both analytic and anecdotal evidence, to be the core group of LSD users: adolescent white males, frequently from relatively advantaged backgrounds. At least for LSD use, therefore, these surveys are probably fairly representative of the population of LSD users.

Drug Abuse Warning Network (DAWN)

The Drug Abuse Warning Network,[9, 10] sponsored by NIDA until 1992 and then by SAMHSA, monitors medical examiners' and coroners' offices and hospital emergency rooms in major metropolitan areas across the country. Its primary goals are to identify hazards associated with drug abuse, to detect new drugs and drug combinations, and to provide data for planning. Although the network has been in existence since 1976, prior to 1990 DAWN data represented only the hospitals that participated. Assessment of trends over time thus was limited to the ever-diminishing group of emergency rooms (ERs) that reported throughout a given time period. In 1989, DAWN changed the method used to select hospitals for participation. Using statistical adjustment of the data submitted by the sample of ERs, DAWN began to produce weighted estimates in 1990 of the total number of drug abuse ER episodes and mentions for the coterminous United States and for twenty-one metropolitan areas.

DAWN data are collected weekly from emergency room departments that provide service seven days a week, twenty-four hours a day, and are located in nonfederal, short-term general hospitals. Each hospital determines its own DAWN data collection procedure. Patients' medical records are reviewed and abstracted by ER or other hospital (or nonhospital) staff. DAWN data are generally collected at the end of a day; thus, if information about drug use is not available on the day of the ER visit (for example, from a delayed toxicology screen, or because the patient is alone and unconscious), that patient would not be included in the DAWN data.

A DAWN *drug abuse episode* must meet several criteria:

- The patient was treated in the hospital's emergency department
- The patient was at least six years old and less than ninety-eight years old
- The patient's problem was induced by or related to drug abuse
- The case involved nonmedical use of a legal drug or use of an illegal drug
- The patient took the drug(s) intentionally either because of dependence, in a suicide attempt or gesture, or for the psychic effects of the drug(s)

Cases in which alcohol was the only substance involved are not reported to DAWN, nor are cases involving accidental ingestion of a substance.

A DAWN *drug abuse mention* refers to the individual drugs named as contributing to a drug abuse episode. Up to four substances in addition to alcohol may be reported for each episode. Mention of a drug does not imply that the specific drug caused the episode.

Cause and effect are difficult to establish using DAWN data. In about half the drug-related emergency room visits reported, the person has taken more than one drug.[6] Thus an adverse reaction or death cannot be directly attributed to a particular drug. Also, a person may appear in the emergency room several or many times. This will tend to inflate estimates of the occurrence of these problems in the general population.

Drug Use Forecasting Project (DUF)

The Drug Use Forecasting Project,[11] sponsored by the National Institute of Justice, investigates drug use among arrestees in twenty-one cities across the United States. The cities are not representative of any broader population. DUF has been collecting data since 1987. Data are collected in voluntary anonymous interviews and from analysis of urine specimens collected at the time of arrest. Arrestees are sampled four times a year over two-week periods. The number of male arrestees charged with drug offenses is restricted so that the sample will include a broad range of arrest charges. Persons charged with drug offenses are more likely to have been using drugs at the time of arrest, however, and DUF probably underestimates some drug use statistics for men. All female arrestees are included regardless of offense.

DUF data are frequently reported in the substance abuse literature, although standard reports are not published. The raw data are available on public-use tape to investigators.*

Community Epidemiology Work Group (CEWG)

The Community Epidemiology Work Group[120] was established by NIDA in 1976 as a method for keeping abreast of the rapidly changing drug scene. Representatives of about twenty metropolitan areas meet twice yearly to monitor patterns and trends in drug use, and to identify new areas of concern. Proceedings of its conferences are published by NIDA. The CEWG reports primarily on measures of the harmful effects of drug abuse. Data sources include DAWN and DUF; state public health agencies; treatment programs; seizure, price, purity, and arrest data from the DEA and state and local law enforcement agencies; and data collected by other sources or in research surveys.

---

*DUF data were made available to the authors by the Data Resources Program of the National Institute of Justice, Sociometrics Corp., 170 State St., Suite 260, Los Altos, CA 94022-2812. The study entitled *The Drug Use Forecasting Project* was conducted by the National Institute of Justice, 633 Indiana Ave., Washington, DC 20531. Funding support for preparing the revised documentation was provided by a contract ((OJP)-89-C-008) between the U.S. Office of Justice Programs and Sociometrics Corp. The original investigators, funding agency, and the Data Resources Program are not responsible for the analyses or interpretations presented here.

Notes

1. Seligmann J, Mason M, Annin P, Marszalek D, Wolfberg A (1992). The new age of Aquarius: LSD, favorite drug of '60s hippies and flower children, is turning on a new generation of American teenagers in the '90s. *Newsweek*, Feb 3, pp 66–67.
2. Treaster JB (1991). Use of LSD, drug of allure and risk, is said to rise. *New York Times*, Dec 27, p A15.
3. Colburn D (1991). LSD: A potent trip. Acid's effects are still a stunning puzzle. *Washington Post Health*, Washington, DC, Sep 24, p 7.
4. Drug Enforcement Administration (1991). It never went away: LSD, a sixties drug, attracks young users in the nineties. US Dept. of Justice.
5. Kleber HD (1967). Prolonged adverse reactions from unsupervised use of hallucinogenic drugs. *J nerv ment dis* 144(4), 308–319.
6. Johnston LD, O'Malley PM, Bachman JG (1993). *National Survey Results on Drug Use From the Monitoring the Future Study, 1975–1992: Vol. I. Secondary School Students*. NIH Pub. No. 93-3597. US Government Printing Office, Washington DC.
7. Substance Abuse and Mental Health Services Administration (1993). *National Household Survey on Drug Abuse: Main Findings 1991*. DHHS Pub. No. (SMA) 93-1980. US Government Printing Office, Washington DC.
8. Johnston LD, O'Malley PM, Bachman JG (1993). *National Survey Results on Drug Use from the Monitoring the Future Study, 1975–1992: Vol. II College Students and Young Adults*. NIH Pub. No. 93-3598. US Government Printing Office, Washington DC.
9. National Institute on Drug Abuse (1992). *Annual Emergency Room Data 1991: Data from the Drug Abuse Warning Network*. Statistical Series I, Number 11-A. DHHS Pub. No. (ADM) 92-1955. US Government Printing Office, Washington DC.
10. National Institute on Drug Abuse (1992). *Annual Medical Examiner Data 1991: Data from the Drug Abuse Warning Network*. Statistical Series I, No. 11-B. DHHS Pub. No. (ADM) 92-1955. US Government Printing Office, Washington DC.
11. National Institute of Justice (1991). *The Drug Use Forecasting Project: 1989*. (Data Set J100, J. L. Peterson & U. A. Colella (Archivists)) [machine-readable

data file and documentation]. Sociometrics Corp., Data Resources Program of the National Institute of Justice, Los Altos, CA (Distributor).

12. Hofmann A (1983). *LSD, My Problem Child: Reflections on Sacred Drugs, Mysticism, and Science.* J. P. Tarcher, Los Angeles.

13. Hofmann A (1975). The chemistry of LSD and its modifications. In: Sankar DVS, ed. *LSD: A Total Study.* PJD Publications Ltd, Westbury, NY. Pp 107–139.

14. Stoll WA (1947). [LSD-25: A hallucinatory agent of the ergot group.] *Schweiz arch neurol* 60, 279–323.

15. Busch AK, Johnson WC (1950). LSD-25 as an aid in psychotherapy (preliminary report of a new drug). *Dis nerv syst* 11, 241–243.

16. Grinspoon L, Bakalar JB (1979). *Psychedelic Drugs Reconsidered.* Basic Books, NY.

17. Yensen R (1985). LSD and psychotherapy. *J psychoactive drugs* 17(4), 267–277.

18. Lee MA, Shlain B (1985). *Acid Dreams: The CIA, LSD and the Sixties Rebellion.* Grove Press, NY.

19. Cohen S, Ditman KS (1962). Complications associated with lysergic acid diethylamide (LSD-25). *JAMA* 181(2), 161–162.

20. Cashman J (1966). *The LSD Story.* Fawcett Publications, Greenwich, CT.

21. Sankar DVS, ed (1975). *LSD: A Total Study.* PJD Publications, Westbury NY.

22. Stevens J (1987). *Storming Heaven: LSD and the American Dream.* Harper & Row, NY.

23. Ulrich RF, Patten BM (1991). The rise, decline, and fall of LSD. *Perspect biol med* 34(4), 561–578.

24. Stafford P (1982). The LSD family (the archetype). In: *Psychedelics Encyclopedia,* rev. ed. J. P. Tarcher, Los Angeles. Pp 35–65.

25. JAMA (1966). Prolonged adverse reactions to LSD [editorial]. *JAMA* 198(6), 658.

26. Krippner S (1985). Psychedelic drugs and creativity. *J psychoactive drugs* 17(4), 235–245.

27. Holden C (1980). Arguments heard for psychedelics probe [news]. *Science* 209(4453), 256–257.

28. Kurland AA (1985). LSD in the supportive care of the terminally ill cancer patient. *J psychoactive drugs* 17(4), 279–290.

29. Strassman RJ (1991). Human hallucinogenic drug research in the United States: A present-day case history and review of the process. *J psychoactive drugs* 23(1), 29–38.

30. Arora RC, Meltzer HY (1989). Increased serotonin$_2$ (5-HT$_2$) receptor binding as measured by ^{3}H-lysergic acid diethylamide (^{3}H-LSD) in the blood platelets of depressed patients. *Life sci* 44(11), 725–734.

31. Cowen PJ, Geaney DP, Schächter M, Green AR, Elliott JM (1986). Desipramine treatment in normal subjects: Effects on neuroendocrine responses to tryptophan and on platelet serotonin (5-HT)-related receptors. *Arch gen psychiatry* 43(1), 61–67.

32. Elliott JM, Kent A (1989). Comparison of [^{125}I]iodolysergic acid diethylamide

binding in human frontal cortex and platelet tissue. *J neurochem* 53(1), 191–196.

33. McBride PA, Mann JJ, Polley MJ, Wiley AJ, Sweeney JA (1987). Assessment of binding indices and physiological responsiveness of the 5-HT$_2$ receptor on human platelets. *Life sci* 40(18), 1799–1809.

34. Norman TR, Judd FK, Staikos V, Burrows GD, McIntyre IM (1990). High-affinity platelet [^{3}H]LSD binding is decreased in panic disorder. *J affective disord* 19(2), 119–123.

35. Palacios JM, Probst A, Cortes R (1983). The distribution of serotonin receptors in the human brain: High density of [^{3}H]LSD binding sites in the raphe nuclei of the brainstem. *Brain res* 274(1), 150–155.

36. Pandey GN, Pandey SC, Janicak PG, Marks RC, Davis JM (1990). Platelet serotonin-2 receptor sites in depression and suicide. *Biol psychiatry* 28(3), 215–222.

37. Schächter M, Geaney DP, Grahame-Smith DG, Cowen PJ, Elliott JM (1985). Increased platelet membrane [^{3}H]-LSD binding in patients on chronic neuroleptic treatment. *Br j clin pharmacol* 19(4), 453–457.

38. Jaffe JH (1990). Drug addiction and drug abuse. In: Goodman LS, Gilman A, eds. *The Pharmacological Basis of Therapeutics*, 8th ed. Pergamon Press, New York. Pp 522–572.

39. Isbell H, Belleville RE, Fraser HF, Wikler A, Logan CR (1956). Studies on lysergic acid diethylamide (LSD-25): I. Effects in former morphine addicts and development of tolerance during chronic intoxication. *Arch neurol psychiatry* 76, 468–478.

40. Berne RM, Levy MN, eds. (1988). *Physiology*. C.V. Mosby, St. Louis, MO.

41. Jacobs BL (1987). How hallucinogenic drugs work. *Am sci* 75, 386–392.

42. Glennon RA (1990). Do classical hallucinogens act as 5-HT$_2$ agonists or antagonists? *Neuropsychopharmacology* 3(5/6), 509–517.

43. Pierce PA, Peroutka SJ (1989). Hallucinogenic drug interactions with neurotransmitter receptor binding sites in human cortex. *Psychopharmacology (Berl)* 97(1), 118–122.

44. Pierce PA, Peroutka SJ (1990). Antagonist properties of *d*-LSD at 5-hydroxytryptamine$_2$ receptors. *Neuropsychopharmacology* 3(5/6), 503–508.

45. Sadzot B, Baraban JM, Glennon RA, Lyon RA, Leonhardt S, Jan CR, Titeler M (1989). Hallucinogenic drug interactions at human brain 5-HT$_2$ receptors: Implications for treating LSD-induced hallucinogenesis. *Psychopharmacology (Berl)* 98(4), 495–499.

46. Titeler M, Lyon RA, Glennon RA (1988). Radioligand binding evidence implicates the brain 5-HT$_2$ receptor as a site of action for LSD and phenylisopropylamine hallucinogens. *Psychopharmacology (Berl)* 94(2), 213–216.

47. Winter JC, Rabin RA (1988). Interactions between serotonergic agonists and antagonists in rats trained with LSD as a discriminative stimulus. *Pharmacol biochem behav* 30(3), 617–624.

48. Eells JT, Wilkison DM (1989). Effects of intraocular mescaline and LSD on visual-evoked responses in the rat. *Pharmacol biochem behav* 32(1), 191–196.

49. Evarts EV, Landau W, Freygang W Jr., Marshall WH (1955). Some effects of

lysergic acid diethylamide and bufotenine on electrical activity in the cat's visual system. *Am j physiol* 182, 594–598.

50. Synder SH, Reivich M (1966). Regional localization of lysergic acid diethylamide in monkey brain. *Nature* 209(5028), 1093–1095.

51. Rosenthal SH (1964). Persistent hallucinosis following repeated administration of hallucinogenic drugs. *Am j psychiatry* 121, 238–244.

52. Hoffer A (1964). *D*-Lysergic acid diethylamide (LSD): A review of its present status. *Clin pharmacol ther* 6, 183–255.

53. Wallace JE, Blum K, Singh JM (1974). Determination of drugs in biologic specimens—a review. *Clin toxicol* 7(5), 477–495.

54. Papac DI, Foltz RL (1990). Measurement of lysergic acid diethylamide (LSD) in human plasma by gas chromatography/negative ion chemical ionization mass spectrometry. *J anal toxicol* 14(3), 189–190.

55. Jaffe JH, Martin WR (1990). Opioid analgesics and antagonists. In: Goodman LS, Gilman A, eds. *The Pharmacological Basis of Therapeutics*, 8th ed. Pergamon Press, New York. Pp. 485–521.

56. Rothlin E (1957). Lysergic acid diethylamide and related substances. *Ann N Y Acad Sci* 66, 668–676.

57. West LJ, Pierce CM, Thomas WD (1962). Lysergic acid diethylamide: Its effects on a male Asiatic elephant. *Science* 138, 1100–1103.

58. Griggs EA, Ward M (1977). LSD toxicity: A suspected cause of death. *J Ky Med Assoc* 75(4), 172–173.

59. Fysh RR, Oon MCH, Robinson KN, Smith RN, White PC, Whitehouse MJ (1985). A fatal poisoning with LSD. *Forensic sci int* 28(2), 109–113.

60. Freedman DX (1968). On the use and abuse of LSD. *Arch gen psychiatry* 18(3), 330–347.

61. Clark WG (1987). Changes in body temperature after administration of antipyretics, LSD, delta^9-THC and related agents: II. *Neurosci biobehav rev* 11(1), 35–96.

62. Brown RT, Braden NJ (1987). Hallucinogens. *Pediatr clin North Am* 34(2), 341–347.

63. Cohen S (1985). LSD: The varieties of psychotic experience. *J psychoactive drugs* 17(4), 291–296.

64. Stedman TL (1990). *Stedman's Medical Dictionary*. Williams & Wilkins, Baltimore.

65. Cytowic RE, Wood FB (1982). Synesthesia: I. A review of major theories and their brain basis. *Brain cogn* 1(1), 23–35.

66. Cytowic RE (1982). Synesthesia and mapping of subjective sensory dimensions [editorial]. *Neurol* 39, 849–850.

67. Rizzo M, Eslinger PJ (1989). Colored hearing synesthesia: An investigation of neural factors. *Neurol* 39, 781–784.

68. Johnson DAW (1981). Drug-induced psychiatric disorders. *Drugs* 22(1), 57–69.

69. Unger SM (1963). Mescaline, LSD, psilocybin, and personality change: A review. *Psychiatry* 26(2), 111–125.

70. Hartung JR, McKenna SA, Baxter JC (1970). Body image and defensiveness in an LSD-taking subculture. *J proj tech pers assess* 34(4), 316–323.

71. Rinkel M, de Shon HJ, Hyde RW, Solomon HC (1952). Experimental schizophrenia-like symptoms. *Am j psychiatry* 108, 572–578.

72. Klee GD (1963). Lysergic acid diethylamide (LSD-25) and ego functions. *Arch gen psychiatry* 8, 461–474.

73. Schmiege GR (1963). The current status of LSD as a therapeutic tool—a summary of the clinical literature. *J Med Soc NJ* 60, 203–207.

74. van Rhijn CV (1960). Introductory remarks: Participants. In: Abramson HA, ed. *The Use of LSD in Psychotherapy: Transactions of a Conference.* Josiah Macy Jr. Foundation Publications, New York.

75. Bender L (1966). D-lysergic acid in the treatment of the biological features of childhood schizophrenia. *Dis nerv syst* 7 Suppl(7), 43–46.

76. Fisher G (1970). The psycholytic treatment of a childhood schizophrenic girl. *Int j soc psychiatry* 16(2), 112–130.

77. Simmons JQ, Benor D, Daniel D (1972). The variable effects of LSD-25 on the behavior of a heterogeneous group of childhood schizophrenics. *Behav neuropsychiatry* 4(1/2), 10–16.

78. Rolo A, Krinsky LW, Abramson H, Goldfarb L (1965). Preliminary method for study of LSD with children. *Int j neuropsychiatry* 1(6), 552–555.

79. Abramson HA (1967). The use of LSD (*d*-lysergic acid diethylamide) in the therapy of children (a brief review). *J asthma res* 5(2), 139–143.

80. Simmons JQ 3d, Leiken SJ, Lovaas OI, Schaeffer B, Perloff B (1966). Modification of autistic behavior with LSD-25. *Am j psychiatry* 122(11), 1201–1211.

81. Brandrup E, Vanggaard T (1977). LSD treatment in a severe case of compulsive neurosis. *Acta psychiatr Scand* 55(2), 127–141.

82. Leonard HL, Rapoport JL (1987). Relief of obsessive-compulsive symptoms by LSD and psilocin [letter]. *Am j psychiatry* 144(9), 1239–1240.

83. Sandison RA, Whitelaw JDA (1957). Further studies in the therapeutic value of lysergic acid diethylamide in mental illness. *J ment sci* 103, 332–343.

84. Smith CG (1969). Gilles De La Tourette syndrome treated with LSD. *Ir j med sci* 8(6), 269–271.

85. Itil TM, Keskiner S, Holden JM (1969). The use of LSD and ditran in the treatment of therapy resistant schizophrenics (symptom provocation approach). *Dis nerv syst* 30(2), 93–103.

86. Kuromaru S, Okada S, Hanada M, Kasahara Y, Sakamoto K (1967). The effect of LSD on the phantom limb phenomenon. *J lancet* 87(1), 22–27.

87. Fanciullacci M, Bene ED, Franchi G, Sicuteri F (1977). Phantom limb pain: Sub-hallucinogenic treatment with lysergic acid diethylamide (LSD-25). *Headache* 17(3), 118–119.

88. Ball JR, Armstrong JJ (1961). The use of LSD 25 in the treatment of the sexual perversions. *Can Psychiatric Asso j* 6, 231–235.

89. Geert-Jörgensen E, Hertz M, Knudsen K, Kristensen K (1964). LSD-treatment: Experience gained within a three-year period. *Acta psychiatr Scand* 40 (Suppl 180), 373–382.

90. Geert-Jörgensen E (1968). Further observations regarding hallucinogenic treatment. *Acta psychiatr Scand* 44 (Suppl 203), 195–200.

91. Johnsen G (1964). Three years' experience with the use of LSD as an aid in psychotherapy. *Acta psychiatr Scand* 40 (Suppl 180), 383–388.

92. Shagass C, Bittle RM (1967). Therapeutic effects of LSD: A follow-up study. *J nerv ment dis* 144(6), 471–478.

93. Kast E (1966). LSD and the dying patient. *Chic Med Sch q* 26(2), 80–87.

94. Pahnke WN, Kurland AA, Goodman LE, Richards WA (1969). LSD-assisted psychotherapy with terminal cancer patients. *Curr psychiatr ther* 9, 144–152.

95. Grof S, Goodman LE, Richards WA, Kurland AA (1973). LSD-assisted psychotherapy in patients with terminal cancer. *Int pharmacopsychiatry* 8(3), 129–144.

96. Grieco A, Bloom R (1981). Psychotherapy with hallucinogenic adjuncts from a learning perspective. *Int j addict* 16(5), 801–827.

97. Ditman KS, Whittlesey JRB (1959). Comparison of the LSD-25 experience and delirium tremens. *Arch gen psychiatry* 1, 47–57.

98. Smart RG, Storm T (1964). The efficacy of LSD in the treatment of alcoholism. *Q j stud alcohol* 25, 333–338.

99. Mottin JL (1973). Drug-induced attenuation of alcohol consumption. A review and evaluation of claimed, potential or current therapies. *Q j stud alcohol* 34, 444–472.

100. Buckman J (1968). LSD in psychiatric therapy. *Curr psychiatr ther* 8, 100–109.

101. Pos R (1968). LSD as an adjuvant to psychotherapy. *Curr psychiatr ther* 8, 115–120.

102. Cohen S, Krippner S (1985). LSD in retrospect. Editor's introduction. *J psychoactive drugs* 17(4), 213–217.

103. Grinspoon L, Bakalar JB (1986). Can drugs be used to enhance the psychotherapeutic process? *Am j psychother* 40(3), 393–404.

104. Riedlinger T, Riedlinger J (1986). Taking birth trauma seriously. *Med hypotheses* 19(1), 15–25.

105. Soskin RA, Grof S, Richards WA (1973). Low doses of dipropyltryptamine in psychotherapy. *Arch gen psychiatry* 28, 817–821.

106. Ungerleider JT, Andrysiak T (1981). Therapeutic uses of the drugs of abuse. *Ann N Y Acad Sci* 362, 173–180.

107. Drug Enforcement Administration (1991). *LSD: A Situation Report*. US Dept. of Justice, November.

108. Giannini AJ, Price WA, Giannini MC (1986). Contemporary drugs of abuse. *Am fam physician* 33(3), 207–216. [Published erratum in *Am fam physician* 1986 33(5):43].

109. Schwartz RH, Comerci GD, Meeks JE (1987). LSD: Patterns of use by chemically dependent adolescents. *J pediatr* 111(6 Pt 1), 936–938.

110. Materson BJ, Barrett-Connor E (1967). LSD "mainlining": A new hazard to health. *JAMA* 200(12), 1126–1127.

111. Solursh LP, Clement WR (1968). Use of diazepam in hallucinogenic drug crises. *JAMA* 205(9), 644–645.

112.National Narcotics Intelligence Consumers Committee (1991). *The NNICC Report 1990: The Supply of Illicit Drugs to the United States*. Drug Enforcement Administration, June.

113.Cheek FE, Newell S, Joffe M (1970). Deceptions in the illicit drug market. *Science* 167(922), 1276.

114.Dumars KW Jr. (1971). Parental drug usage: Effect upon chromosomes of progeny. *Pediatrics* 47(6), 1037–1041.

115.Barron SP, Lowinger P, Ebner E (1970). A clinical examination of chronic LSD use in the community. *Compr psychiatry* 11(1), 69–79.

116.Smith DE, Rose AJ (1968). The use and abuse of LSD in Haight-Ashbury (observations by the Haight-Ashbury Medical Clinic). *Clin pediatr (Phila)* 7(6), 317–322.

117.Ungerleider JT, Fisher DD, Fuller M, Caldwell A (1968). The "bad trip": The etiology of the adverse LSD reaction. *Am j psychiatry* 124(11), 1483–1490.

118.Beck J (1992). Personal communication.

119.Drug Enforcement Administration (1991). *Illegal Drug Price/Purity Report: United States Calendar Year 1988 through June 1991*. No. DEA-91004. US Dept. of Justice, November.

120.Community Epidemiology Work Group (1992). *Epidemiologic Trends in Drug Abuse: Proceedings, December 1991*. DHHS Pub. No. (ADM)92-1918. US Government Printing Office, Washington DC.

121.American Psychiatric Association (1987). *Diagnostic and Statistical Manual of Mental Disorders (DSM-III-R)*. American Psychiatric Association, Washington DC.

122.Cohen S (1960). Lysergic acid diethylamide: Side effects and complications. *J nerv ment dis* 130, 30–40.

123.Cohen SA (1966). A classification of LSD complications. *Psychosomatics* 7(3), 182–186.

124.Tietz W (1967). Complications following ingestion of LSD in a lower class population. *Calif med* 107(5), 396–398.

125.Robbins E, Frosch WA, Stern M (1967). Further observations on untoward reactions to LSD. *Am j psychiatry* 124(3), 393–395.

126.Milman DH (1967). An untoward reaction to accidental ingestion of LSD in a 5-year-old girl. *JAMA* 201(11), 821–825.

127.Reed CF, Witt PN (1965). Factors contributing to unexpected reactions in two human drug-placebo experiments. *Confin psychiatr* 8(2), 57–68.

128.Greenblatt DJ, Shader RI (1970). Adverse effects of LSD: A current perspective. *Conn med* 34(12), 895–902.

129.Ditman KS, Tietz W, Prince BS, Forgy E, Moss T (1968). Harmful aspects of the LSD experience. *J nerv ment dis* 145(6), 464–474.

130.Decker WJ, Brandes WB (1978). LSD misadventures in middle age [letter]. *J forensic sci* 23(1), 3–4.

131.Smith DE, Seymour RB (1985). Dream becomes nightmare: Adverse reactions to LSD. *J psychoactive drugs* 17(4), 297–303.

132.Naditch M (1975). Relation of motives for drug use and psychopathology in the development of acute adverse reactions to psychoactive drugs. *J abnorm psychol* 84, 374–385.

133. Naditch MP (1974). Acute adverse reactions to psychoactive drugs, drug usage, and psychopathology. *J abnorm psychol* 83(4), 394–403.

134. Naditch MP (1975). Ego functioning and acute adverse reactions to psychoactive drugs. *J pers* 43(2), 305–320.

135. Naditch MP, Alker PC, Joffe P (1975). Individual differences and setting as determinants of acute adverse reactions to psychoactive drugs. *J nerv ment dis* 161(5), 326–335.

136. Cohen S (1974). Psychodysleptic drugs: Adverse reactions. In: Radouco TS, ed. *Pharmacologie, toxicologie, et abus des psychotomimétiques (hallucinogènes)*. Les Presses de l'Université Laval, Quebec. Pp 315–319.

137. Malleson N (1971). Acute adverse reactions to LSD in clinical and experimental use in the United Kingdom. *Br j psychiatry* 118(543), 229–230.

138. Fink M, Simeon J, Haque W, Itil T (1966). Prolonged adverse reactions to LSD in psychotic subjects. *Arch gen psychiatry* 15(5), 450–454.

139. Keeler MH (1967). Lysergic acid diethylamide. Adverse reactions and use in experimental therapy. *N C med j* 28(8), 323–327.

140. Bewley TH (1967). Adverse reactions from the illicit use of lysergide. *Br med j* 3(556), 28–30.

141. Smart RE, Bateman K (1967). Unfavorable reactions to LSD: A review and analysis of the available case reports. *Can Med Assoc j* 97(20), 1214–1221.

142. Hamzepour S (1968). Lysergic acid diethylamide (LSD) overdose complicated by Mendelson's syndrome. *Br j clin pract* 22(10), 436–438.

143. Cooper HA (1955). Hallucinogenic drugs [letter]. *Lancet* 1, 1078–1079.

144. Elkes C, Elkes J, Mayer-Gross W (1955). Hallucinogenic drugs [letter]. *Lancet* 1, 719.

145. Ungerleider JT, Fisher DD, Fuller M (1966). The dangers of LSD: Analysis of seven months' experience in a university hospital's psychiatric service. *JAMA* 197(6), 389–392.

146. Shick JFE, Smith DE (1970). Analysis of the LSD flashback. *J psychedelic drugs* 3(1), 13–19.

147. Hoffer A (1972). LSD-induced psychosis and vitamin B_3 [letter]. *Am j psychiatry* 128(9), 1155.

148. Peters G (1970). A study of psychedelic drug users. *Schizophrenia* 2, 103–108.

149. McGlothlin WH, Arnold DO (1971). LSD revisited: A ten-year follow-up of medical LSD use. *Arch gen psychiatry* 24(1), 35–49.

150. Hensala JD, Epstein LJ, Blacker KH (1967). LSD and psychiatric inpatients. *Arch gen psychiatry* 16(5), 554–559.

151. Forrest JAH, Tarala RA (1973). 60 hospital admissions due to reactions to lysergide (LSD). *Lancet* 2(841), 1310–1313.

152. Fisher DD, Ungerleider JT (1968). The therapy of untoward LSD reactions. *Curr psychiatric ther* 8, 110–114.

153. Blacker KH (1970). Aggression and the chronic use of LSD. *J psychedelic drugs* 3(1), 32–37.

154. Taylor RL, Maurer JI, Tinklenberg JR (1970). Management of "bad trips" in an evolving drug scene. *JAMA* 213(3), 422–425.

155. Hungerford DA, Taylor KM, Shagass C, LaBadie GU, Balaban GB, Paton GR (1968). Cytogenetic effects of LSD-25 therapy in man. *JAMA* 206(10), 2287–2291.

156. Abraham HD, Aldridge AM (1993). Adverse consequences of lysergic acid diethylamide. *Addiction* 88(10), 1327–1334.

157. Khantzian EJ, McKenna GJ (1979). Acute toxic and withdrawal reactions associated with drug use and abuse. *Ann intern med* 90(3), 361–372.

158. Kulberg A (1986). Substance abuse: Clinical identification and management. *Pediatr clin North Am* 33(2), 325–361.

159. Eisner BG, Cohen S (1958). Psychotherapy with lysergic acid diethylamide. *J nerv ment dis* 127, 528–539.

160. Matefy RE, Hayes C, Hirsch J (1978). Psychedelic drug flashbacks: Subjective reports and biographical data. *Addict behav* 3, 165–178.

161. Matefy RE, Krall RG (1974). An initial investigation of the psychedelic drug flashback phenomena. *J consult clin psychol* 42(6), 854–860.

162. Naditch MP, Fenwick S (1977). LSD flashbacks and ego functioning. *J abnorm psychol* 86(4), 352–359.

163. Ungerleider JT, Fisher DD, Goldsmith SR, Fuller M, Forgy E (1968). A statistical survey of adverse reactions to LSD in Los Angeles County. *Am j psychiatry* 125(3), 352–357.

164. Blumenfield M (1971). Flashback phenomena in basic trainees who enter the U.S. Air Force. *Milit med* 136, 39–41.

165. Horowitz MJ (1969). Flashbacks: Recurrent intrusive images after the use of LSD. *Am j psychiatry* 126(4), 565–569.

166. Moskowitz D (1971). Use of haloperidol to reduce LSD flashbacks. *Milit med* 136(9), 754–756.

167. Stanton MD, Bardoni A (1972). Drug flashbacks: Reported frequency in a military population. *Am j psychiatry* 129(6), 751–755.

168. Stanton MD, Mintz J, Franklin RM (1976). Drug flashbacks: II. Some additional findings. *Int j addict* 11(1), 53–69.

169. Abraham HD (1983). Visual phenomenology of the LSD flashback. *Arch gen psychiatry* 40(8), 884–889.

170. Abraham HD (1982). A chronic impairment of colour vision in users of LSD. *Br j psychiatry* 140, 518–520.

171. Frosch WA, Robbins ES, Stern M (1965). Untoward reactions to lysergic acid diethylamide (LSD) resulting in hospitalization. *N Engl j med* 273(23), 1235–1239.

172. Saidel DR, Babineau R (1976). Prolonged LSD flashbacks as conversion reactions. *J nerv ment dis* 163(5), 352–355.

173. Anderson WH, O'Malley JE (1972). Trifluoperazine for the trailing phenomenon [letter]. *JAMA* 220(9), 1244–1245.

174. Kaminer Y, Hrecznyj B (1991). Lysergic acid diethylamide-induced chronic visual disturbances in an adolescent. *J nerv ment dis* 179(3), 173–174.

175. Smith DE (1968). Acute and chronic toxicity of marijuana. *J psychedelic drugs* 2, 37–47.

176. Tennant FS, Groesbeck CJ (1972). Psychiatric effects of hashish. *Arch gen psychiatry* 27, 133–136.

177.Weil AT (1970). Adverse reactions to marihuana: Classification and suggested treatment. *N Engl j med* 282(18), 997–1000.

178.Thurlow HJ, Girvin JP (1971). Use of antiepileptic medication in treating "flashbacks" from hallucinogenic drugs. *Can Med Assoc j* 105(9), 947–948.

179.Heaton RK (1975). Subject expectancy and environmental factors as determinants of psychedelic flashback experiences. *J nerv ment dis* 161(3), 157–165.

180.Schwarz CJ (1967). Paradoxical responses to chlorpromazine after LSD. *Psychosomatics* 8, 210–211.

181.Hollister LE (1962). Drug-induced psychoses and schizophrenic reactions: A critical comparison. *Ann N Y Acad Sci* 96, 80–92.

182.Abraham HD (1980). Psychiatric illness in drug abusers [letter]. *N Engl j med* 302(15), 868–869.

183.Esecover H, Malitz S, Wilkens B (1961). Clinical profiles of paid normal subjects volunteering for hallucinogen drug studies. *Am j psychiatry* 117, 910–915.

184.Cohen S, Ditman KS (1963). Prolonged adverse reactions to lysergic acid diethylamide. *Arch gen psychiatry* 8, 475–480.

185.Rosenberg CM, Eldred B (1968). LSD psychosis. *Med j Aust* 55, 129–131.

186.Schwarz CJ (1968). The complications of LSD: A review of the literature. *J nerv ment dis* 146(2), 174–186.

187.Hatrick JA, Dewhurst K (1970). Delayed psychosis due to LSD. *Lancet* 2(676), 742–744.

188.Dewhurst K, Hatrick JA (1972). Differential diagnosis and treatment of lysergic acid diethylamide induced psychosis. *Practitioner* 209(251), 327–332.

189.Glass GS (1973). Psychedelic drugs, stress, and the ego. The differential diagnosis of psychosis associated with psychotomimetic drug use. *J nerv ment dis* 156(4), 232–241.

190.Strassman RJ (1984). Adverse reactions to psychedelic drugs: A review of the literature. *J nerv ment dis* 172(10), 577–595.

191.Weintraub W, Silberstein AB, Klee GD (1959). The effect of LSD on the associative processes. *J nerv ment dis* 128, 409–414.

192.Blacker KH, Jones RT, Stone GC, Pfefferbaum D (1968). Chronic users of LSD: The "acidheads." *Am j psychiatry* 125(3), 341–351.

193.Vardy MM, Kay SR (1983). LSD psychosis or LSD-induced schizophrenia? A multimethod inquiry. *Arch gen psychiatry* 40(8), 877–883.

194.Tucker GJ, Quinlan D, Harrow M (1972). Chronic hallucinogenic drug use and thought disturbance. *Arch gen psychiatry* 27, 443–447.

195.Breakey WR, Goodell H, Lorenz PC, McHugh PR (1974). Hallucinogenic drugs as precipitants of schizophrenia. *Psychol med* 4, 255–261.

196.Fuller DG (1976). Severe solar maculopathy associated with the use of lysergic acid diethylamide (LSD). *Am j ophthalmol* 81(4), 413–416.

197.Schatz H, Mendelblatt F (1973). Solar retinopathy from sun-gazing under the influence of LSD. *Br j ophthalmol* 57(4), 270–273.

198.Ewald RA (1971). Sun gazing associated with the use of LSD. *Ann ophthalmol* 3(1), 15–17.

199. Rosen DH, Hoffman AM (1972). Focal suicide: Self-enucleation by two young psychotic individuals. *Am j psychiatry* 128(8), 1009–1012.

200. Sotiropoulos A (1974). Injury to the bladder: Unusual complication of lysergic acid diethylamide. *Urology* 3(6), 755–758.

201. Smith RN, Robinson K (1985). Body fluid levels of lysergide (LSD). *Forensic sci int* 28(3–4), 229–237.

202. Williams LN (1969). LSD and manslaughter. *Lancet* 2(615), 332.

203. Barter JT, Reite M (1969). Crime and LSD: The insanity plea. *Am j psychiatry* 126(4), 531–537.

204. Knudsen K (1964). Homicide after treatment with lysergic acid diethylamide. *Acta psychiatr Scand* 40 (Suppl 180), 389–395.

205. Reich P, Hepps RB (1972). Homicide during a psychosis induced by LSD. *JAMA* 219(7), 869–871.

206. Klock JC, Boerner U, Becker CE (1973). Coma, hyperthermia and bleeding associated with massive LSD overdose: A report of eight cases. *West j med* 120(3), 183–188.

207. Lieberman AN, Bloom W, Kishore PS, Lin JP (1974). Carotid artery occlusion following ingestion of LSD. *Stroke* 5(2), 213–215.

208. Sobel J, Espinas O, Friedman S (1971). Carotid artery obstruction following LSD capsule ingestion. *Arch intern med (Chicago)* 127, 290–291.

209. Choi YS, Pearl WR (1989). Cardiovascular effects of adolescent drug abuse. *J adolesc health care* 10(4), 332–337.

210. Alldredge BK, Lowenstein DH, Simon RP (1989). Seizures associated with recreational drug abuse. *Neurol* 39, 1037–1039.

211. Fisher DD, Ungerleider JT (1967). Grand mal seizures following ingestion of LSD[25]. *Calif med* 106(3), 210–211.

212. Mercieca J, Brown EA (1984). Acute renal failure due to rhabdomyolysis associated with use of a straitjacket in lysergide intoxication. *Br med j* 288(6435), 1949–1950.

213. Brody SL, Wrenn KD, Wilber MM, Slovis CM (1990). Predicting the severity of cocaine-associated rhabdomyolysis [see comments]. *Ann emerg med* 19(10), 1137–1143.

214. Bakheit AMO, Behan PO, Prach AT, Rittey CD, Scott AJ (1990). A syndrome identical to the neuroleptic malignant syndrome induced by LSD and alcohol [letter]. *Br j addict* 85(1), 150–151.

215. Behan WMH, Bakheit AMO, Behan PO, More IAR (1991). The muscle findings in the neuroleptic malignant syndrome associated with lysergic acid diethylamide. *J neurol neurosurg psychiatry* 54(8), 741–743.

216. Friedman SA, Hirsch SE (1971). Extreme hyperthermia after LSD ingestion. *JAMA* 217(11), 1549–1550.

217. Liskow B (1971). Extreme hyperthermia from LSD [letter]. *JAMA* 218(7), 1049.

218. Grant I, Mohns L (1975). Chronic cerebral effects of alcohol and drug abuse. *Int j addict* 10(5), 883–920.

219. Kornblith AB (1981). Multiple drug abuse involving nonopiate, nonalcoholic

substances: II. Physical damage, long-term psychological effects and treatment approaches and success. *Int j addict* 16(3), 527–540.

220. Wright M, Hogan TP (1972). Repeated LSD ingestion and performance on neuropsychological tests. *J nerv ment dis* 154(6), 432–438.

221. McGlothlin WH, Arnold DO, Freedman DX (1969). Organicity measures following repeated LSD ingestion. *Arch gen psychiatry* 21(6), 704–709.

222. McGlothlin W, Cohen S, McGlothlin MS (1970). Long lasting effects of LSD on normals. *J psychedelic drugs* 3(1), 20–31.

223. Abraham HD, Wolf E (1988). Visual function in past users of LSD: Psychophysical findings. *J abnorm psychol* 97(4), 443–447.

224. Cohen MM, Marinello MJ, Back N (1967). Chromosomal damage in human leukocytes induced by lysergic acid diethylamide. *Science* 155(768), 1417–1419.

225. Dishotsky NI, Loughman WD, Mogar RE, Lipscomb WR (1971). LSD and genetic damage: Is LSD chromosome damaging, carcinogenic, mutagenic, or teratogenic? *Science* 172(3982), 431–440.

226. Long SY (1972). Does LSD induce chromosomal damage and malformations? A review of the literature. *Teratology* 6, 75–90.

227. Egozcue J, Irwin S (1970). LSD-25 effects on chromosomes: A review. *J psychedelic drugs* 3(1), 10–12.

228. Robinson JT, Chitham RG, Greenwood RM, Taylor JW (1974). Chromosome aberrations and LSD: A controlled study in fifty psychiatric patients. *Br j psychiatry* 125, 238–244.

229. Poland BJ, Wogan L, Calvin J (1972). Teenagers, illicit drugs and pregnancy. *Can Med Assoc j* 107, 955–958.

230. Golbus MS (1980). Teratology for the obstetrician: Current status. *Obstet gynecol* 55(3), 269–277.

231. Cohen MM, Shiloh Y (1977). Genetic toxicology of lysergic acid diethylamide (LSD-25). *Mutat res* 47(3/4), 183–209.

232. McGlothlin WH, Sparkes RS, Arnold DO (1970). Effect of LSD on human pregnancy. *JAMA* 212(9), 1483–1487.

233. Margolis S, Martin L (1980). Anophthalmia in an infant of parents using LSD. *Ann ophthalmol* 12(12), 1378–1381.

234. Siffroi JP, Viguie F, Romani F (1988). Unstable translocation t(14;21) in a man, inherited as a t(13;14) in one of his daughters. *Clin genet* 34(1), 15–19.

235. Tenorio GM, Nazvi M, Bickers GH, Hubbird RH (1988). Intrauterine stroke and maternal polydrug abuse: Case report. *Clin pediatr (Phila)* 27(11), 565–567.

236. Beall JR (1973). A teratogenic study of four psychoactive drugs in rats. In: Abstracts of Papers Presented at the Second Meeting of the European Teratology Society, Prague, Czechoslovakia, May 23–26, 1972. *Teratology* 8, 214–215.

237. Emerit I, Roux C, Feingold J (1972). LSD: No chromosomal breakage in mother and embryos during rat pregnancy. *Teratology* 6(1), 71–73.

238. Wilson JG (1973). Present status of drugs as teratogens in man. *Teratology* 7, 3–15.

239. Kandel DB (1982). Epidemiological and psychosocial perspectives on adolescent drug use. *J Am Acad Child Psychiatry* 21(4), 328–347.

240. Kandel DB, Logan JA (1984). Patterns of drug use from adolescence to young adulthood: I. Periods of risk for initiation, continued use, and discontinuation. *Am j public health* 74(7), 660–666.

241. Stead AH, Watton J, Goddard CP, Patel AC, Moffat AC (1986). The development and evaluation of a ^{125}I radioimmunoassay for the measurement of LSD in body fluids. *Forensic sci int* 32(1), 49–60.

242. Castro A, Malkus H (1977). Radioimmunoassays of drugs of abuse in humans: A review. *Res commun chem pathol pharmacol* 16(2), 291–309.

243. Altunkaya D, Smith RN (1990). Evaluation of a commercial radioimmunoassay kit for the detection of lysergide (LSD) in serum, whole blood, urine and stomach contents. *Forensic sci int* 47(2), 113–121.

244. Blum LM, Carenzo EF, Rieders F (1990). Determination of lysergic acid diethylamide (LSD) in urine by instrumental high-performance thin-layer chromatography. *J anal toxicol* 14(5), 285–287.

245. McCarron MM, Walberg CB, Baselt RC (1990). Confirmation of LSD intoxication by analysis of serum and urine. *J anal toxicol* 14(3), 165–167.

246. Paul BD, Mitchell JM, Burbage R, Moy M, Sroka R (1990). Gas chromatographic-electron-impact mass fragmentometric determination of lysergic acid diethylamide in urine. *J chromatogr* 529(1), 103–112.

247. Francom P, Andrenyak D, Lim HK, Bridges RR, Foltz RL, Jones RT (1988). Determination of LSD in urine by capillary column gas chromatography and electron impact mass spectrometry. *J anal toxicol* 12(1), 1–8.

248. Lim HK, Andrenyak D, Francom P, Foltz RL, Jones RT (1988). Quantification of LSD and N-demethyl-LSD in urine by gas chromatography/resonance electron capture ionization mass spectrometry. *Anal chem* 60(14), 1420–1425.

249. Bowen JM, McMorrow HA, Purdie N (1982). Quantitative determination by circular dichroism of lysergic acid diethylamide in confiscated material. *J forensic sci* 27(4), 822–826.

250. National Criminal Justice Association (1991). *A Guide to State Controlled Substances Acts*. National Criminal Justice Association, Washington DC.

251. Newton J (1992). Tough sentences in LSD cases decried. *Los Angeles Times*, July 27.

252. Johnson D (1993). For drug offenders, how tough is too tough? *New York Times*, Nov 8, p A16.

253. Paton SM, Kandel DB (1978). Psychological factors and adolescent illicit drug use: Ethnicity and sex differences. *Adolescence* 13(50), 187–200.

254. Robinson TN, Killen JD, Taylor CB, Telch MJ, Bryson SW, Saylor KE, Maron DJ, Maccoby N, Farquhar JW (1987). Perspectives on adolescent substance use: A defined population study. *JAMA* 258(15), 2072–2076.

255. Jones AP (1973). Personality and value differences related to use of LSD-25. *Int j addict* 8(3), 549–557.

256. Smart RG, Jones D (1970). Illicit LSD users: Their personality characteristics and psychopathology. *J abnorm psychol* 75(3), 286–292.

257.Page RM (1990). Shyness and sociability: A dangerous combination for illicit substance use in adolescent males? *Adolescence* 25(100), 803–806.

258.Ludwig AM, Levine J (1965). Patterns of hallucinogenic drug abuse. *JAMA* 191(2), 92–96.

Index